Resurrection Life Now!

Activating Resurrection Life In You!

Rudi Louw

Most Scripture quotations are taken from the *Revised Standard Version*, Holy Bible, Thomas Nelson Publishers. Copyright © 1983 by Thomas Nelson, Inc.

Some Scripture quotations were taken from the *New King James Version*, Holy Bible, Thomas Nelson Publishers. Copyright © 1983 by Thomas Nelson, Inc.

All Scripture quotations not taken from the RSV, NKJV are a literal translation of the Scriptures.

The Holy Scriptures are just that, HOLY.

Statements enclosed in brackets were inserted into Scripture quotations to add emphasis or clarify the meaning of what is being said in those scriptures. The integrity of God's Word to man was not compromised in any way. Due care and diligence was cautiously exercised to keep the Word of Truth intact.

For example, the apostle Paul said in his second letter to Timothy in chapter three verse sixteen that: *"All Scripture is given by inspiration of God* (literally God breathed)*, and is profitable for doctrine, for reproof, for correction, for instruction **in righteousness**,"* NKJV

Content

The marvel of the Holy Bible

1. The *theme* and *inspired thought* of Scripture continues *uninterrupted*.

It took *1,500 years* to compile the Holy Bible, involving *more than 40 different authors*, yet the theme and inspired thought of Scripture continues *uninterrupted*, from author to author, from beginning till end.

2. *Absence* of mythical stories:

Compare philosophies and theories about creation in the Middle East, Europe, Asia, Africa and Latin America, and you'll find mythical scenarios, gods feuding and cutting up other gods to form the heavens and the earth. In ancient Greek mythology, the Greeks see Atlas carrying the earth on his shoulders. In India, Hindus believe 8 elephants carry the earth on their backs.

But in contrast, Job, the oldest book in the Holy Bible, declares that *God suspends the earth 'on nothing.'* (Job 26:7)

This was said millennia before Isaac Newton discovered the invisible laws of gravity that delicately balance every planet and sun in its individual circuit.

In contrast to every other ancient attempt to give a creation account, *the Holy Bible pictures the creation of the earth in a truly scientific manner.*

In Gen 1 for instance, the continents are lifted from the seas, then vegetation is formed and later, animal life, all reproducing *'according to its own kind,'* **thus recognising the fixed genetic laws.**

Finally, we have the bringing forth of man and woman, *all done by God in a dignified and proper manner, without mythological adornments.*

The rest of the Holy Bible follows suite.

The narratives are **true historical documents,** *faithfully reflecting society and culture,* **as history and archaeology would discover them thousands of years later. Not only is the Holy Bible historically accurate, it is also reliable when it deals with scientific subjects.**

It was not written as a textbook on history, science, mathematics or medicine, *yet, when its writers touch on these subjects, **they often state facts that scientific advancement would not reveal or even consider until thousands of years later.***

While many have doubted the accuracy of the Holy Bible, time and continued research have consistently demonstrated that the Word of God is better informed than its critics.

3. The Holy Bible is *intact*.

Of all the ancient works of substantial size, *the Holy Bible against all odds and expectations survives intact.*

Compared with other ancient writings, the Holy Bible has more manuscripts as evidence to support it than any ten pieces of classical literature combined!

The plays of William Shakespeare, for instance, were written about four hundred years ago, and written after the invention of the printing press. Many of his original words have been lost in numerous sections, *yet the Holy Bible's uncanny preservation has weathered thousands of years of wars, contradictions, persecutions, fires and invasions.*

*Jewish scribes, **like no other manuscript has ever been preserved**, preserved the Holy Bible's Old Covenant text through centuries. **They kept tabs on every letter, syllable, word and paragraph**.*

*They continued from generation to generation to appoint and train distinct classes of men within their culture **whose sole duty it was to preserve and transmit these documents <u>with perfect accuracy and fidelity</u>**.*

Who ever bothered to count the letters, syllables, or words of Plato, Aristotle or Seneca for that matter?

When it comes to the New Testament, the actual number of preserved manuscripts is so numerous that it becomes overwhelming.

There are more than 5,680 Greek manuscripts, more than 10,000 Latin Vulgate manuscripts and at least 9,300 other versions; there exist a further 25,000 manuscript copies of portions of the New Testament.

No other document of antiquity even begins to approach such numbers.

The closest in comparison is Homer's <u>Iliad</u> with only 643 manuscripts. The first complete work of Homer only dates back to the 13th century.

4. In dealing with time, the Holy Bible *accurately foretells what will happen ahead of time, with unmatched results*.

No other ancient work even begins to attempt this.

Other books claim divine inspiration, such as the Koran, the Book of Mormon, and parts of the Veda. ***But none of these books contains predictive foretelling.***

This one fact we know for certain, and it is undeniable: *While microscopic scrutiny would show up the imperfections, blemishes and defects of any work of man, <u>it magnifies the beauties and perfection of God</u>, just as every flower displays in accurate detail, the reflection and perfection of beauty, <u>so does the Word of Truth when it is scrutinized</u>.*

Historian, Philip Schaff wrote:

'*...Without money and weapons, Jesus the Christ conquered more millions than Alexander, Caesar, Mohammed and Napoleon. Without science and learning, He (Jesus the Christ) shed more light on things human and divine than all philosophers and scholars combined.*

Without the eloquence of schools, He (Jesus the Christ) spoke such words of life as was never spoken before or since and produced effects, which lie beyond the reach of orator or poet.

*Without writing a single line, He (Jesus the Christ) set more pens in motion, and furnished themes for more sermons, orations, discussions, learned volumes, works of art, and songs of praise, **than the whole army of great men of ancient and modern times combined**.'* (The person of Christ, p33. 1913)

Today, there are literally billions of Bibles in more than 2,000 languages,

...isn't it about time you find out what it really has to say?

Hey listen, the Holy Bible is all about Jesus, the Messiah, the Christ,

...and everything about Jesus Christ is really about YOU!!

Study Tips:

Read 2Corinthians 5:14, 16, 18, 19, and 21.

In the light of these Scriptures it should be obvious that if you want to study the Holy Bible,

…you should study it in the light of mankind's Redemption!

Daily feed on Redemption Realities, found in the book of Acts, Romans 1 through 8, Ephesians, Colossians, Galatians, 1Peter 1, 2Peter 1, James 1, 1 and 2Corinthians.

Acknowledgement

I want to acknowledge and thank one of my mentors in the faith, Francois du Toit, for blessing and impacting my life with revelation knowledge.

The portion on *"The marvel of the Holy Bible"* was borrowed from his website: http://www.mirrorword.net/ as students so often feel they have a right to do with things that come from teachers they respect. Just as Galatians 6:6 says: *"Let him who is taught the Word **share in all good things** with him who teaches."*

To all our dear friends and family, and those who helped me with this project,

…but especially to my wife Carmen:

For all the love and support,

THANK YOU!

Foreword

Thank you for taking the time to read this book.

Let me start off by saying that I am totally addicted to my Daddy's love for me; I am in love with Jesus Christ, *and that is enough for me!*

The love of God is so much more than a doctrine, a philosophy, or a theory; it is so much more and goes so much deeper than knowledge; it way surpasses knowledge,

…we are talking heart language here,

…therefore this book was not written to impress intellectuals with knowledge and philosophy, theologians with theories and doctrine, nor English majors with grammar and spelling for that matter,

…so if you come up with any other definitions or find any language inaccuracies, please don't use it to disqualify Love's own message I bring to you in this book.

I write *to impact people's hearts;*

…to make them see the mysteries that have been hidden in Father God's heart, concerning Christ Jesus, and really *concerning THEM,* so as to arrest their conscience with it, *that I may introduce them to their original design, and to their true selves;* **and present them to themselves perfect in Christ Jesus,**

*…and set them apart unto Him **in love**, as a* chaste virgin,

We are involved with the biggest romance of the ages;

…therefore this book cannot be read as you would a novel; *casually.* It is not a cleverly devised little myth or fable.

It contains revelation and *truth* into some things you may or may not have considered before. It is not blasphemy or error though.

It is the TRUTH of God, ultimate TRUTH, and therefore has direct bearing upon YOUR life,* the Word and the Spirit is my witness *to the reality of these things!

Be like the people of Berea the apostle Paul ministered to in Acts 17:11. Open yourself up to study the revelation contained in this book, *to see if these things are **true and real**.*

*…but be forewarned, do not become guilty of the sins of the Pharisees, **or you too will miss out on the depth of fulfillment God Himself, who is LOVE, wants to give you**.*

(Jesus said of the Pharisees and Sadducees that they strain out every little gnat BUT swallow whole camels. What He meant by that is that *some people seem to have it all together when it comes to doctrine and they love to argue.*

It makes them feel important, but it is nothing other than EMPTY religious and intellectual pride.

*They know the Scriptures in and out, and YET they are still so IGNORANT about **REAL TRUTH that is only found in LOVE;***

…they are still so ignorant and indifferent **towards the things that REALLY MATTERS.**

They are always arguing over the use of *every little jot and tittle* and over the meaning and interpretation of *every word of Scripture.*

The exact thing they accuse everyone else of doing though; the precise thing they judge everyone else for, *they are actually doing themselves,* that is: **they often downright misinterpret and twist what is being said, *making a big deal of insignificant things,***

…while obscuring or weakening God's real truth; the truth of His LOVE

They are always majoring on minors, **<u>because they do not understand the heart of God</u>**

...and therefore they constantly miss the whole point of the message.)

Paul himself said it so beautifully:

*"...the letter kills but **the Spirit BRINGS LIFE**;"*

*"...<u>knowledge puffs up</u>, but **LOVE EDIFIES**."*

I say again:

Allow yourself to get caught up in the revelation I am about to share.

Open yourself up to study the insight contained in this book, *not only with a desire to gain knowledge, but also with anticipation **to hear from Father God yourself**;*

*...**to encounter Him through His Word**;*

*...**and to embrace truth, in order to know and believe the LOVE God has for <u>you</u>**,*

*...so that you may get so caught up in it **that you too may receive from Him; LOVES' impartation of LIFE***

This revelation contains within it the voice and call of LOVE Himself to every human being on the face of this earth.

If you take heed to it, it is custom designed and guaranteed, to forever alter and enrich your life!

"There is therefore now no condemnation to those who are in Christ Jesus"

"For the law of the Spirit of life in Christ Jesus has set me free from the law of sin and death"

"For God did

what the Law, weakened by the flesh, could never do.

He sent forth His Son in the likeness of sinful flesh

to be a sin offering.

He condemned sin in the flesh,"

"...so that the righteous requirement of the Law might be fulfilled in us,

who do not live according to the flesh,

but according to the Spirit!"

~ Romans 8:1-4

Prayer

Father, I thank you that you dip the fine wheat of your bread into honey.

Father, we are conscious of the nourishment we receive *as Your Word enters in,*

…and we do not ever want to develop a callousness towards Your Word;

…a hardness Father.

We want to be quick to hear; quick to obey Lord.

Thank you for Your precious Word, Father.

Thank you for Your truth, *and the impact of that truth upon our hearts.*

And Father, we know that as we, even in this book, touch Your precious incorruptible seed today; Your precious abiding Word; the incorruptible seed of Your life, *that there will be explosions in our spirit Lord,*

…explosions of life and of joy,

…and a release from anything that can possibly bind us up and restrict us and hold us

back from giving full expression of that Zoë life we see and encounter in Your Word.

Thank you that You are equipping us, Father, as part of a team You are raising up,

…You are equipping us, as an army of people *who are able to walk in the power of Your might, and in Your glory,*

…**through the power of God,**

…**through the working of God within us.**

And, we do not want to deceive ourselves, Father, *by putting any confidence in the flesh,*

…**but we put our confidence, in the working of Your Word and Your Spirit, on the inside of us.**

And we are here in this moment, ready to listen to You, in Your Word, and in this book!

We are hungry Father, not to be schooled by man, but to be schooled by the Holy Spirit.

We recognize and acknowledge His ability to teach.

We understand that He is commissioned *to lead us into all truth.*

And Father, we want to be sensitive to Him and follow His logic and His lead *as He instructs us through truth.*

Holy Spirit, speak to us even in this book, in Jesus Name!

We will be equipped, we will be strengthened, we will be edified, and we will be motivated,

…so that Your zeal may freely burn within us,

…so that we may go out and get the job done,

…that job, that God Himself has given us, in the great commission,

…in Jesus Name!

Amen.

Chapter 1

Now in Christ Jesus

Let's start in Romans chapter eight.

We are discovering some priceless truth in these days, and I want to share it with you, because you may be able to buy this book, but what I am eager to share, I tell you, *you can't buy these truths with money,*

…**because the truth of this revelation is so powerful, that it sets you free, *to set others free!***

So open your ears to hear, because this is what God desires: *that He may equip you, to in turn equip others;*

…not just so that you might be blessed, *but so that you might be a blessing to others God sends your way,* **and also to the ones He sends you to**.

Romans 8:1

*"There is therefore, <u>**now,**</u> **no condemnation**…"*

Yes, **NOW!**

Now that we no longer live under the old system; the Law; *that Law **that brought the knowledge of sin**;*

*…**that brought the focus upon sin**,*

…and *with that knowledge, **and that emphasis,*** it also brought *condemnation and guilt,*

…thus, it not only exposed sin, **but fueled it,** *to become something beyond measure;*

*…an out of control fire, with no stop to it, which **scorches and kills everything!***

With the knowledge of the Law, *we also discovered **the law of sin, and death.***

We realize that the Law says: *"You shall not!"*

*…*but, within that same context, *we discovered that within the members of our bodies, **there was a stronger law, which was in existence already,***

…and it declared war with that Law we tried to embrace in our minds; *we discovered that it was at war with the Law of our minds,*

I mean, we could learn the Law of God off by heart, *and we could know it in our minds, **but while the law of sin dominated within us, death reigned;***

...it REIGNED!

And that death, which reigned, *caused us to obey the lusts of the flesh,*

...it caused us to obey the prince of the power of the air, and **we could not** *obey the Law.*

BUT NOW, IN CHRIST JESUS, this fight **has ended,** and,

"There is therefore, NOW,
NO CONDEMNATION"

Hallelujah!

Romans 8:1

"There is therefore, NOW..."

(...**now that that old Law system is done away with**),

"...there is **THEREFORE,** *NOW,*
no condemnation for those who are in Christ Jesus!"

Some translations add there:

"...For those that walk not after the flesh but after the Spirit,"

...but it is not found in the earlier, older manuscripts.

The younger manuscripts added it in there, repeating verse four,

…but it is an unnecessary redundancy, *and it is not accurate according to the earlier manuscripts, **and it only tends to add confusion rather than clarity.***

Romans 8:2

"For the law of the Spirit, of, life in Christ Jesus, has set me free, from the law of sin and death.*"*

That word, *"law"* used there, refers to, **government being in place.**

The term, *"law"* always refers and points to *a* **government** of some sorts, *a governing authority; a governing influence or power.*

So, Romans 8:2 can be read as saying:

*"…the government of the Spirit; or the governing influence of the Spirit; or the governing power of the Spirit, **has set me free** from the government, the governing influence; the governing power of sin and death"*

Let's quickly look at that government of sin and death in Romans five, before we move on here in Romans chapter eight.

Chapter 2

The law of sin and death

Romans 5:17

"If because of one man's trespass, death reigned, through that one man…"

Verse 14 says,

"…yet death reigned, from Adam to Moses, even over those whose sins were not like the transgression of Adam"

Verse 13 goes on to say,

"Sin was indeed in the world, before the Law was given, but sin is not calculated (…sin is not measured accurately) *where there is no Law"*

"…yet death reigned!"

So, even though sin wasn't calculated accurately; even though sin wasn't counted, before the Law was given; even though the guy didn't know it was wrong to do it; *"…yet death reigned"*

Death reigned!

That's why the Law had to be introduced,

…because God wanted to reveal sin; *reveal what it is;*

…*and at the same time* **expose sin for what it actually leaves us with,**

…**so that, that reign and the dominion of death, through the law of sin, can be broken**

You see, before the Law of Moses could even be introduced, *that law of sin and death was already in operation.*

That government of sin and its fruit, the dominion of death, *has been in operation since Adam.*

It began to operate in the fall of Adam; *in Adam's fall.*

That government came into operation there.

And then the Law was given through Moses, and in that Law God introduced His will to Israel, *and then to the rest of the world through Israel.*

God introduced His will to man, **to expose sin.**

You see, in Romans seven it says,

 "Before the Law was given, we did not know it was wrong to covet, but now all of a sudden,

the Law says: 'You shall not covet!' **and Sin found opportunity***…"*

Let's read it there, (You are welcome to read it in your own Bible if you like).

Romans 7:7

"What shall we say then, that the Law is sin?

By no means! If it had not been for the Law, I would not have known sin.*"*

"I discovered that, Sin, finding opportunity in the commandment, worked (or brought about) *in me, all kinds of covetousness."*

So, the government of Sin, and therefore, death, was there all the time;

…the rule of Sin was there all the time,

…but it deceived me; it lied to my conscience,

…I thought I was okay, I thought I wasn't doing anything wrong, okay, maybe a little, but it wasn't that bad! Everybody else is like this, so I'm alright; I'm okay; I'm just fine!

The Bible says: *"…it deceived me…"*

Romans 7:11

"For, Sin, finding opportunity in the commandment, deceived me, and by it, killed me."

Chapter 3

What gave the law of sin and death its power?

Let's get back to verse two of Romans eight.

Romans 8:2

"For the law of the Spirit (…the government of the Spirit of Life; that life I now enjoy; that life in Christ Jesus; that life that was revealed in Him and then given to me,) **has set me free** *from the law of sin and death* (…from that government of Sin, and of death)*"*

What gave that government its power?

I mean, what gave the law of sin and death its power?

What made it a law in my life?

…because you must agree, *that law* **had something behind it** which fueled it, and gave it energy …it gave it power over me.

It became some kind of government, *and actually had, some even greater government, behind it,* **that actually *forced you, to do* the exact thing that you hate to do**,

…because now you have received the Law, and the Law says:

"You shall not, you shall not; you shall NOT!

…you shall, you shall; you SHALL!"

…and I've discovered what the Law says, *and within my inner man, I agree with that Law; I agree that the Law is good.*

With my mind I accept that the Law is good, but I find in my members, in that same member of my mind, in those same faculties of my mind and the members of my body, a law, *in existence already,* a law, *which is contrary to that Law,*

…I find that there is a warfare going on inside of me, *in the faculties of my mind; in my spirit, in my very members, in my very body,*

…there is a war raging within me; a war between that which is good, and this law, *this government of Sin that forces me to do the wrong thing.*

So, obviously there was **another government**; **some other, even greater power,** *behind the law of sin and death.*

What was that power?

What was that government?

What was that thing?

Where does the enemy get that authority and power from to bind me?

From my ignorance!

From Adam originally,

…from the ignorance;

…from the lies,

…from the deception,

…I inherited from him,

*…but I want you to see that the enemy is empowered, **through my ignorance!***

He is empowered, *through that ignorance I received through Adam.*

It was passed on to me *from Adam.*

You see, originally, way back there in the beginning,

…Adam was blessed with dominion, originally.

God blessed Adam with it.

God gave Adam dominion.

The devil was cast out of Heaven.

He didn't have any dominion.

He is a fallen angel.

He was below the angels.

He was a cast-out.

But then, *through his lies and deception,*

…through the deception he created, he caused Adam to fall.

He took Adam's dominion away from him.

He took Adam's dominion, *when he manipulated him and caused him* to transgress God's word.

You see, that dominion originally given to Adam; *Adam's own dominion, **now gave Satan power.***

Adam gave him power to operate in.

*I want you to see that he uses **Adam's own dominion,***

*…**through the devil's manipulation and control of Adam, he used Adam's dominion.***

So, in the spirit dimension, ***Adam gave Satan dominion,*** *spiritually and naturally,*

…because everything in the natural, is being upheld, in the spirit dimension.

In the spirit realm, in reality, **Adam gave the devil dominion,**

…to operate and exercise that dominion *on the earth;*

…in the spirit realm, and in the natural realm.

Thus, Adam through Satan's manipulation, gave away **his dominion.**

He gave **his dominion** to the devil.

I want you to see and understand this clearly:

The devil, through manipulation, through his deception, caused Adam to fall, and then he took over **Adam's own dominion;** and thus, he took Adam's dominion from him.

He for all intents and purposes manipulated Adam's dominion, and thus took control of Adam's dominion, and that's what then gave the devil, the dominion, the power to operate here on planet earth.

In 2Corinthians 4:4, the devil is called,

"…the god of this world"

In Luke 4:5-6 the devil took Jesus and showed Him all the kingdoms of the world, in a moment of time, and he said to Him:

*"To you I will give all this authority and their glory, **for it has been delivered over to me,** and I give it to whom I will. If then you will worship me, it shall be yours"*

(Just as a side note: It is interesting to note that every temptation that the enemy tempted Jesus with, was not just a questioning of His identity, but a temptation to avoid the cross, and to take a shortcut to His destiny.

Through the cross, Jesus was going to redeem all these things;

…through the cross, Jesus was going to reach His destiny, and have every one of these things the devil tempted Him with, and so He refused to take a shortcut, and be led astray.

I thank God, that through the cross, the kingdoms of this world, have become the kingdom of our God, and of His Christ!)

You see, the enemy knew, he already anticipated, that the Seed of the women was going to crush his authority, and crush his headship …the head of the serpent,

…but here in Luke, we have a particularly interesting statement:

*"…**all this has been delivered over to me**"*

Who delivered all that authority and all that glory to the devil?

Adam did!

In the fall, through Satan's manipulation and his deception, Adam delivered all that authority to the devil,

…all that authority **that God gave <u>him</u>.**

Satan, through His deception, manipulated Adam's authority and caused Adam to fall, and He then took Adam's authority, and Adam's dominion, when he caused Adam to transgress God's word.

You see, if Satan did not **take Adam captive,** *through his lies, through strong deception,* **if he did not have Adam's authority; manipulated Adam's dominion,** *the law of sin and death would be powerless.*

It would be powerless!

If I didn't inherit that deception from Adam;

…that ignorance,

…if Satan did not have Adam's authority and Adam's dominion, *Adam's influence,* over me,

…if he did not manipulate and have Adam's dominion, then he would have no power over men;

…then the law of sin and death would not have any power over me,

…***it would be powerless!***

Listen, if it was not a real government,

…if Satan's lies and deception **was not a real power,**

…if it was not a real powerful **governing influence,**

…if the law of sin and death was not **a real power,**

…**a real government,**

…then the Law of Moses would be good enough to keep us straight,

…it would be good enough, in its knowledge it brings you, of what is good, and what is bad,

…and with that knowledge of what is good, people should be able to do what is good you see...

But we are not just dealing with the law of sin and death here,

…otherwise that knowledge of what is good, that is presented to me in the Law of Moses, *should be enough to break us free from the sin; from that death,* **but it can't!**

Because you see, *we are not just dealing with mere sin and death.*

That law of sin and death **has a greater governing force,**

*…a greater governing **power** behind it.*

It has government behind it,

…it has authority behind it,

…it has power behind it,

…because its powerful influence was given to Satan, **through the embrace of deception**,

…through the embrace of the lie, and confusion and ignorance,

…through that embrace of Satan's deception,

"Sin entered into the world, through one man,

…and death through sin"

"The sting of death is sin"

That one little initial sting;

…that initial little sin,

…that embrace of that initial little lie, and manipulation and deception,

…brought the law of sin and death into the world;

…it brought death into the world,

…and that death spread to all men,

…*that sin and death.*

Thus, Satan, through Adam's fall, got all men to sin and come under the dominion of death, and the reign, and the government, of the law of sin and death.

Do you see that this is what needed to be dealt with in Christ?

…in the incarnation?

…in the cross?

Not just the law of sin and death; that government that sin and death has over humanity,

…but that government that sin and death has *through the lie,*

…through that deception that was introduced to humanity, in Adam, and through Adam

*That government of the **lie;** that government of **ignorance and deception;** that government and power and influence that Sin has upon the human race **must be broken.***

It must be broken!

If it's not broken, *then man will continue to be **a slave of sin!***

You can make a person as religious as you want to,

…**but if you cannot break the government of the <u>lie</u> and of <u>ignorance</u> and <u>deception</u>; the government of sin and death,**

…then in his life, sin will continue to reign!

Where deception <u>reigns</u>,

…where ignorance and confusion and deception and darkness <u>reigns</u>,

…where <u>that death</u> <u>reigns</u>,

….man will continue to be separated from God!

I mean, *he will <u>remain</u> separated from God!*

And then sin and death will also *continue to reign* in his life!

Chapter 4

The law of the Spirit of life in Christ Jesus

We are discovering, in this book, *the power that is behind the law of the Spirit of life in Christ Jesus.*

What makes that law powerful?

I mean, we could just say, let's start a new law,

…let's all just start driving on the opposite side of the road than the side we are now used to driving on,

…but, that just would be a powerless law

I mean, *if there is nothing behind that law,*

…no strong government,

…to enforce that law,

…then it would simply be *a powerless law,*

…**it would just be a totally powerless law!**

What makes the law of the Spirit of life in Christ Jesus so powerful?

In Ephesians 1, Paul prays for us,

…he prays that God would,

"…enlighten us,"

…that God would,

"…open the eyes of our heart,"

"…the ears of our understanding,"

…**enlighten them!**

*"…with a spirit of wisdom and revelation **into the knowledge of Him,**"*

*"…**that you may know** what is the living hope, to which He has called you;"*

*"…**that you may know** what are the riches of His glorious inheritance, in the saints."*

Verse 19 says,

*"…and **that you may know** what is **the immeasurable greatness of His power, in us,**"*

*"…**who believe**,"*

"…(exactly) according to the working of His great might,"

"…which He accomplished in Christ,"

"…when He raised Him from the dead,"

"…and made Him sit at His right hand,"

"…in the heavenly realm, (in the unseen dimension of spirit reality)*,"*

"…far above,"

"…all rule,"

"…and authority,"

"…and power,"

"…and dominion,"

"…and above every name"

"…that is named, or can possibly be named."

Now, do you believe that that position, that was given to Jesus,

…because of the power of the working of God's great might in His resurrection,

…do you believe that that position, is a position that is above,

…all rule, and authority, and power, and dominion?

Can you agree with me that it includes the authority and the rule of sin and death?

So then, God gave Jesus an authority and power, that is above *all* rule and authority and dominion,

…including the rule and authority and dominion of death,

…especially the dominion of death!

Now, Jesus did not get that position and dominion, **for His own sake.**

He had that position already!

Jesus, the eternal blueprint Son Himself, was not subject to the government of sin and death.

He did what He did, ***for us!***

So many Christian, religious, man-made doctrines, just continue to look at Jesus, the perfect One, the wonderful One,

…'You're so lovely Jesus. You're so sinless. You're so spotless!'

*…'But shame, poor us, **we're so sinful!**'*

…**and they totally miss the plan of God!**

Why did Jesus do what He did?

He took on flesh and blood, and He went to the cross; _He did it for us_!

*"...**He was wounded,**
for _our_ transgressions,"*

*"...**He was bruised, for _our_ iniquity**"*

He also says exactly that in verse 22 of Ephesians chapter 1,

Ephesians 1:22

"...and He (God the Father) *has put all things under His* (Jesus') *feet, and has made Him, the head over all things, **for the Church**"*

*"...**for the Church!**"*

*"...**for the benefit of the Church!**"*

*"...**which is His body; the fullness of Him**, who fills **all** in **all**.*"

Ephesians 2:6

*"...He made us alive, together with Christ, **and raised us up, with Him, and made us sit, together**, in the heavenly realm, in Christ Jesus* (...in the spirit realm, in the unseen realm of spirit **reality**).*"*

Can you understand now, why there is no condemnation, for those who are in Christ Jesus?

In the light of His crucifixion and resurrection, on behalf of us all, *it is impossible now, in that light, to view Romans 8:1 in an incorrect context.*

I do not understand how anyone can use Romans 8:1 *as an excuse to still continue in sin,* **except through their ignorance!**

All they need to do is follow along and go back with me to Romans 5, *and they will see that there is no room for any of those excuses and arguments of weakness to continue to function.*

Romans 6:1 says,

"What shall we say then?"

"Are we to continue in sin, that grace may abound?"

*"**By no means!**"* he says,

What a stupid argument!

God forbids it!

How can I continue in sin, if I'm seated in Christ Jesus, in the heavenly realm of spirit reality and authority, *far above the* *dominion of that thing* that kept me in death!

It would be the most foolish thing to do!

It would be utter stupidity, *to again submit to an authority that is far beneath you;*

...that is far below your feet!

Especially with the knowledge that that authority is going to *bring me right back into that death I already escaped!*

It would be brainless for me, *to submit and subject myself again to that authority;*

...to submit myself, by choice, to an authority that will kill me!

Jesus Christ introduced a government of life, *through His resurrection!*

...and He raised us up with Him,

...and made us sit with Him,

...in the heavenly realm of spirit reality and authority,

....*far above*,

...all rule,

...and power,

…**and dominion**,

…**and authority of any kind!**

Let's go back to Romans 8.

Chapter 5

Making room for weakness will leave you bound!

Romans 8:1

*"There is, **therefore, <u>now,</u>** no condemnation…"*

You see with a wrong interpretation of Romans 7 we have interpreted this Romans 8:1, as meaning:

'…well, you know chapter 7, it's just a Christian's struggle with his carnal man, with his flesh you know; it's just chronicling the life of an ordinary Christian's struggle with carnality, with sin, in his Christianity,'

'…he knows now that he shouldn't sin, but he still finds himself doing it, and, you know, he will just remain that way, living like that, until Jesus comes back,'

'…and you know, that's just our lot in life,'

'…so let's just not feel guilty,'

'…so let's just not feel too condemned about it,'

'…so Christians, listen man, when you sin, and you know you're going to, I mean all of us sin, even the preacher sins,'

'…so when you sin, just know this fact,'

'…I mean just take comfort in the fact that we all sin man, even the preachers, we all sin man,'

*'…**so don't feel guilty and don't feel too condemned about it**,'*

'…because, praise the Lord, Romans 8:1 says:'

*"**There is therefore now no condemnation, <u>for those</u> who are in Christ Jesus,**"*

*'…for those who **<u>are</u>** in Christ Jesus;'*

*'…**for those who have made it in, those who have prayed the sinner's prayer, and now call themselves Christians,'***

*'…**so, let's not worry about our sin too much, okay!**'*

Hey man, that's <u>deception</u>!

Hey, that's a big fat <u>lie</u>, straight from the pits of Hell!

There's <u>no truth</u> in that doctrine of demons, that have kept, and will continue to keep

many many people in bondage, *if they continue to listen and adhere to it!*

Listen; there is now no condemnation for us, not because I've made it into this very exclusive Christian club, *but because Jesus Christ released me from that government of sin and death, amen!*

"...for the law of the Spirit,"

*....that **spirit law of <u>faith</u>**,*

...that spirit law of,

 *"...**<u>life</u> in Christ Jesus**,"*

...that **faith** and that **life**, *"...**has <u>set me free</u>**,"*

*"...**from <u>the law of sin</u> and death!**"*

Verse 3,

*"**For God <u>has done</u>**..."*

That reminds me of 2Corinthinas 5:17 & 18,

*"**THEREFORE** if any man is in Christ, **he's <u>a new creature</u>**;"*

*"...**the old things <u>have passed away</u>**;"*

*"...**everything <u>has become new</u>**"*

*"...**and <u>all this</u> is from God**"*

It is from <u>God</u>!

It's not some little old Baptist doctrine, or some Methodist, Presbyterian, or Pentecostal Charismatic doctrine, or some church's doctrine…

NO!

"All this is from <u>God</u>, who in Christ Jesus reconciled us to Himself, <u>no longer counting our trespasses against us</u>!"

You see I want you to know, *it is impossible for reconciliation to become* **a practical reality;** *a* **practical** *thing,* **if sin is still an un-dealt-with reality**, working against you, standing between the two of you, *having to be constantly counted and measured and calculated when it comes to you!*

I mean *it will then always be coming between the two of you, against you!*

It will stand in the way of reconciliation and relationship <u>every time</u>, **all the time!**

There can be no genuine friendship in that environment!

It simply won't survive!

…it won't survive!

...it can't exist in such an environment *of sin and constant suspicion and condemnation and guilt!*

Can you see how making even the slightest little bit of room for sin in your doctrine and in your life *will practically cancel out the whole New Covenant?*

You see the devil wants you to look at sin *and not see it as something* **that is really so very bad,**

...but God wants you to see sin *for what it truly is*,

...and He wants you to see and to know *what it actually leaves you with*.

If any one of us want to just conveniently slip into our thinking and into our understanding and into our teaching, **a comfortable little doctrine, to excuse our own failings and sins,** *we cancel the whole Covenant; we cancel that whole New Covenant,* **as far as we are concerned!**

We can't cancel it in Heaven.

It stands secure forever and ever and ever!

But as far as our enjoyment and experience of that Covenant *in the here and now* is concerned,

...*we make it null and void, and cancel it out,*

...**through our wrong thinking and wrong believing and wrong teaching,**

...**and our wrong interpretation *that we have embraced* when it comes to the Scriptures!**

Chapter 6

God has done what the Law could never do!

Romans 8:3

*"**For God has done**…"*

Hallelujah!

He has done it!

*"**For God has done** what the Law (…the Mosaic Law, the Law of Moses) weakened by the flesh, **could never do!**"*

Why was the Law weakened?

I mean, what was in the flesh?

…what was at work there?

….what was working in the flesh?

…what was in that flesh that weakened the Law?

It was a mindset of deception!

…it was the governing influence of sin and death;

…that government,

…that law of sin and death!

You see, the law of sin and death **was so settled and strong <u>in man's mind</u>**,

*…**it had the flesh just where it wanted it.***

It would merely have to **whisper;**

…it would introduce **just one little thought,**

…one little **stimulant,**

…saying: *'**Do** this,'* or, *'**Do** that,'*

…and it would find the flesh, **just ready to do it.**

And God would scream through the Law of Moses,

…Man, **don't** do it! **Don't** do it!

…but the law of sin *in the mind,*

…***<u>that trapped us</u> in a natural dimension,***

*…in **deception;***

*…in **naturally oriented thinking,***

*…fleshly **thinking,***

*…that law, that influence, Sin, **<u>ruling the mind</u>,** **had the body <u>under its government</u>**,*

…and the enemy **just plays with it** like a puppet on a string!

*…and all the time your mind, your better judgment, your inner conscience would scream, **Don't do it!***

…and what happens now,

…now that the Law of Moses came,

…guilt, and inferiority, and condemnation comes,

…do you see that?

BUT NOW, in Christ Jesus, you see,

…now that I'm delivered from the law of sin and death,

…from its dominion over me,

…from it's dominion over my life,

*…hey **there's no condemnation**,*

…**there is now no more condemnation!**

I'm free in Christ Jesus!

I'm liberated in Him!

"You shall <u>know</u> the truth and the truth shall make you <u>free</u>!" – John 8:32

The truth **sets you <u>free</u>!**

Hallelujah!

Amen!

Free as a bird!

Romans 8:3

"For <u>God has done</u> …what the Law <u>could not do</u>…"

<u>God has done it</u>,

"…by sending His Son in the likeness of sinful flesh,"

"…and for sin (…to be that sin offering)"

*"…**He condemned sin in the flesh!**"*

Chapter 7

Bringing many sons to glory!

You see there in Hebrews 2:6-8, he refers to that prophecy of David in Psalm 8:4

"What is man that You are mindful of him? The son of man, that You make so much of him?"

*"You made him a little lower than God ('ELOHIM'), and crowned him with glory and honor, **putting everything in subjection under him;** under his feet"*

It says there in verse 8,

Hebrews 2:8

*"In putting everything in subjection to him, **He left nothing that is not put under man,**"*

*"...**He left nothing outside his control!**"*

See, this is a clear picture of God's man; God's original man,

...that which God originally had in mind,

...what He had in mind for man from the very beginning.

It's a picture of God's man!

...God's design of man!

God placed everything in subjection to man, it is subject to man.

God left nothing outside of the control of man, when God created for man a body, and brought man forth, from within Himself.

God had a man in mind that would walk in dominion.

God did not have a weak failure in mind!

...a defeated old tired and worthless creature!

...a slave creature,

...enslaved to sin!

No!

God had a man in mind, that would walk in dominion, as God's representative here on planet earth!

...a man, that would walk in the glory of God!

...in the glory of God's own image and likeness!

…a man, that would walk in the glory of God's own authority!

*"…**but as yet** …we do not see everything in subjection to him."*

*'…**because of the fall** brother Rudi!'*

Hebrews 2:9

*"**BUT** we see Jesus…"*

*"…**BUT WE SEE JESUS!**"*

"…who for a little while was also made lower than the angels"

(…and here even the original writer of Hebrews got it wrong… ha… ha… ha…

It is correct according to the Greek, but according to the original reference used from Psalm 8 it is incorrectly translated into the Greek.

That original word in the Hebrew is *'ELOHIM'* meaning God.)

"…we see Jesus, who for a little while was made lower than God"

(…because remember, He laid aside His majesty. Jesus emptied Himself of His God attributes, and became a man.)

"…we see Jesus, who for a little while was made lower than God"

"…lower than God (not angels)*,"*

Listen, He could not be made lower than angels, because then He would be made lower than man,

…and man is above angels.

Angels are lower in authority and rank than man.

Amen!

"BUT we see Jesus*,"*

"…He who laid aside His majesty, also for a little while was made lower than God;"

"…(being made a man, never the less, He was) *crowned with glory and honor."*

And the we also see Him,

"Because of the suffering of death,"

*"…**bringing many sons to glory!"***

Hebrews 2:14

"Since therefore*…"*

You see, we see Jesus, and He did what He did; *He went through the suffering of death,* **to release man,**

…**to restore to man** what man lost in the garden.

"Since therefore the children **share** *in flesh and blood,* **He Himself,** <u>**likewise,**</u> **partook of the same**…*"

(…this is talking about Jesus now; He remained in very essence, God, at the core of His being, He still kept the Divine nature, He remained the God who is love, but He laid aside His majesty, His omnipotence, His omniscience, etcetera, and He took on a flesh and blood body.)

"…He Himself, <u>**likewise,**</u> **shared in the same**…*"

"…He, likewise, **partook of the same**"

(In other words, **He partook of flesh and blood, when He became a man,**

…**the same** *flesh and blood body!*)

You see He is spirit.

We are spirit also, ***but we*** <u>***partake***</u> ***of flesh and Blood,*** *for the time we live here on planet earth,*

*…**we partake** of flesh and blood.*

God gave us a body, when He brought us forth out of Himself.

He formed a flesh and blood body, for this being called man, to dwell in, *while he lives here on planet earth.*

Now, in order for God to come and release man…

John 4 says,

"God is spirit,"

…so, in order for God to release man, God had to **partake** of flesh and blood.

In John 1:14 we read that,

"…the Word is spirit,"

…the Son is spirit,

…**but,** that Word **partook** of flesh and blood;

*"…the Word **became flesh!**"*

When Mary conceived, it was the Word that gave birth in her womb, to a child, to a man Jesus,

…He became **flesh and blood,**

…the Son **became flesh and blood;**

…the Word; the 'LOGOS' **became a man;**

….the original authentic blueprint Son **became a man.**

He humbled Himself, He laid aside His majesty, His God attributes, to **partake** of flesh and blood;

…I mean, before He became a man, He was in the glory of God,

…He did not need a physical body;

…the Son; the 'LOGOS,' the Word did not need a physical body, **when He created the world.**

John 1, Colossians 1, and Hebrews 11 say that,

*"…the worlds were created and framed, and is upheld, **by the Word** of His power,"*

…and His Word is spirit.

His Word does not need letters;

…His Word does not need a body;

…His Word was and is spirit and life!

But in order to redeem fallen man, His Word had to **partake** of flesh and blood,

…in order to release man, from the law of sin and death;

…in order to break the dominion of these things;

…in order to break the dominion of that death,

*…**He had to partake of flesh and blood**.*

Hebrews 2:14

*"…He Himself, likewise, **partook of the same**"*

*"…**He shared in the same flesh and blood**"*

And then he says here,

*"…so that, **through death**…"*

Do you see that?

He entered into *that death* we were living in;

…He entered into ***that prison house,* called flesh;**

…and He entered *that realm;*

…into death itself,

(**Now listen acutely carefully**,)

"...in order that He might destroy him..."

I want you to see now, clearly, *what lies behind the law of the Spirit of life*

It is <u>the resurrection</u>, amen!

Chapter 8

Resurrection Power!

The resurrection, is that power, *that brought that law of the Spirit of life, into operation,*

…it was the cause of it.

The resurrection, is *what makes it effective, and gives it authority and power,*

…so that I could *live in it,*

…so I can *live* under the lordship;

…*the superiority,*

…*and the authority,*

…*and the power of that law, amen!*

So, Jesus partook of that death, *and He entered into that realm, into the dominion of death itself,*

"…to destroy him who had the power of death…"

Do you now see how that law of sin and death *could not operate without power behind it?*

...without the father of lies and deception upholding it, with lies and deception,

...**through stolen authority,**

...**stolen power,**

...***through the power and authority and dominion of Adam,***

...**the power, authority, and dominion** *afforded him through Adam,*

...given to him, *by Adam,*

...*Adam **afforded him** that power and authority and dominion,*

...**through ignorance,**

...**the power of ignorance,**

...***through the lie and deception Adam bought into.***

Through the power that *the manipulation, and the lie;* that *deception* had over Adam, over mankind; **the devil was afforded dominion,**

...**he was afforded that power to operate the law of sin and death.**

*Without that, the law of sin and death **could not, and cannot, operate!***

You see that law of sin and death **cannot operate** just because it is a law on a piece of paper,

No!

It operated, because it was <u>a real force</u>!

There was a real government,

…a very real power behind it!

<u>That power</u> had to be destroyed!

But it could only be destroyed by God Himself!

So, God Himself partook of flesh and blood,

…and Jesus was conceived and borne in a womb of a woman;

…He was born on planet earth, from a woman's womb, *in a physical body, <u>just like ours</u>.*

John 1:14 says,

*"…and the Word became flesh, **and we beheld His glory**"*

And then that same Word **partook also** of *death, upon that cross.*

That Word took upon Himself, the curse, of man.

That Word took upon Himself, that death,

…and then that Word also partook of death itself,

…because death is the ultimate conclusion of sin,

…death is the ultimate curse.

He took that death, and He went into the realm of death,

…and He cried the cry of confused and ignorant and deceived humanity,

"My God, my God, why have you forsaken me?"

*He partook of **that death** of being forsaken by God,*

*…experiencing **separation from God**,*

*…being **separated from God**,*

*…**to fully identify with you!***

You see before you can _identify_ with God,
God had to come and _identify_ with you!

...before you can _identify_ with His
resurrection, *He had to come and _identify_*
with your separation,

...and *_that death_ you live in!*

He even had to _literally_ identify with your
literal death,

...the ultimate curse ...the ultimate
separation *from life!*

And so, before we could _identify_ with His
righteousness;

...before we could be _identified by that_
righteousness,

...by His very own righteousness,

...*He had to come and fully _identify_ with our*
sin;

...*He had to be made sin for us, with our*
sin,

...*He even had to be made Sin itself;*

...*_representing_ that whole thing called Sin,*

...and kill it,

...and take it to the grave,

...and bury it there!

"...He, who knew no sin, became sin,"

...we, who knew no righteousness, became righteous!

"...He became Sin, (and sin) *so that* **we** (**in His death and resurrection**) *might become the righteousness of God"* – 2Corinthians 5:21

You, in your very being, may now be the righteousness of God,

...because, **in Him,** **you** were set free!

...because, **in Him,** **you** became the righteousness of God!

...because, **in Him,** **you** were restored to the glory and authority **you** fell from!

...because, **in Him,** **your** original design was redeemed and restored to you,

...the experience of this reality belongs to all those who **believe,** who **embrace** these things!

You are righteousness!

In your very being, you are righteousness!

And you can be that righteousness!

Because of Jesus!

Hallelujah!

Because of Jesus, <u>you</u> can be again that righteousness <u>you</u> were designed to be!

Hallelujah!

But let's get back to Hebrews 2:14 now,

Hebrews 2:14

*"…so that, through death, He might destroy Him, who had the power of death, that is the devil, **and deliver**…"*

Do you see there the result of the destruction of the power of death?

That result is:

YOUR DELIVERANCE!

"…so that, through death, He might destroy Him, who had the power of death, that is the devil,"

*"…**and <u>deliver</u> all those, who through fear of death, were subject to lifelong bondage**"*

Did you catch that?

Do you see how death operated and exercised its authority over man?

Through fear!

(*Ignorance and confusion and deception and darkness* [the fear of the unknown and the undefined], *just adds to fear*)

But what does fear relate to?

What does fear relate to, *in this context of man and God, and the fall?*

Fear relates to punishment!

Chapter 9

We know and believe the Love God has for us!

Let's quickly look at 1John 4 so we can see what God has to say about this.

This teaching, this concept is so supremely essential for us to grasp,

So, read this book again and again if you have to,

Go read these Scriptures for yourself,

Meditate on it, again and again and again, and marinate in it, *until the full revelation of it lives in you!*

1John 4:16-19

*"So, we **know**, and **believe**..."*

...**we are not ignorant and confused and deceived about it anymore, amen!**

*"...so, **we know**, <u>**and believe**</u>, **the love God has for us!**"*

*"…we believe …**the love God has for us.**"*

*"**God is love,**"*

*"…and he **who abides in that love,**"*

*"…**abides** in God, **and God abides in him.**"*

17 *"…**In this** is love **perfected** with us;"*

*"…**so that we may have confidence**"*

"…for the day of judgment."

I know it talks about the day of judgment here,

*…but that judgment can also be related **to an attack** from the enemy, who would just love to see us **suffer.***

*…he is the **accuser** of the brethren, and **he is always judging us,***

*…and trying to trip us up, or snare us, **and then pile upon us, guilt, and shame, and condemnation,***

*…**but**,*

*"…**we may have confidence <u>in that day of attack</u>, because the love of God is perfected in us**;"*

*…**the knowledge of it!***

82

*"…we **know** and **believe** it,"*

…and so <u>we remain secure</u> in our Daddy's love!

"…we know <u>and believe</u> the love God has for us,"

"…so we may have confidence for the day of judgment,"

"…because <u>as He is</u>, so are we, in this world…"

We are identified with Him,

*…we are **in love** with Him,*

…because <u>we have come to realize</u> His love for us!

We love Him, <u>*because He first loved us*</u> you see!

We have come to <u>know</u> these things, and we have become perfected, or <u>*fully persuaded*</u> in it!

And now he says:

1John 4:17

*"<u>**As He is**</u>, <u>**so are we**</u>, in this world!"*

1John 5:20 says,

"We know that the Son of God has come, and **He has given us <u>understanding</u>**, *so we may* **<u>know</u> Him who is true**. *And* **we are in Him** *who is true… in His Son Jesus Christ …He is the true God and eternal life!"*

*"…***we are in Him who is true***…"*

*…***in His death, in His burial, in His resurrection, in His ascension!**

*…***and we've <u>seen it</u>, and <u>believe it</u>, and <u>abide</u> in Him!**

*…***and we have come to <u>know</u>, and <u>believe</u>, we are His kids!**

*…***we have <u>fully identified ourselves</u> with Him!**

*…***and, <u>we are partakers</u> of the divine nature!**

*"…***<u>as He is</u>, <u>so are we</u>, in this world!***"*

Do you think Jesus has confidence?

Sure He does!

Why would He have confidence?

Because sin has no hold on Him!

He doesn't see himself as a sinner!

He sees Himself as sinless,

He's got no sin-consciousness,

He sees sin as <u>defeated</u>,

*…and He **is** sinless,* amen,

He doesn't see sin as an issue, ***because He makes no room for it in His life,***

…**sin is not a part of His identity!**

Sin is not a part of His life!

He is not a sinner, *because it is not a part of His life, **it is not who He is!***

Amen!

And we now are identified with Him,

…**and we now <u>identify ourselves</u> with <u>Him</u>, *and we share in His identity!***

*"…**<u>as He is</u>, <u>so are we</u>, in this world!**"*

Now 1John 4:18 says,

"There is <u>no fear in love</u>, but <u>perfect love</u> casts out all fear!"

Again, where does that perfect love come from?

Verse 16,

"...we __know__, and __believe__, the love God has, for us!"

So, "...__herein is love perfected!__"

Amen!

We have come to __know__ these things,

*...*and we have become __perfected__, or *__fully persuaded__* in it!

And now __we have confidence__, even in the very Day of Judgment!

...because you see, **you cannot begin to enjoy God's love,**

...before you, first, __accept__ the __integrity__ of that love,

...before you, first, __accept__ the love God has, for __you__,

...the __integrity__ of His love, for __you__!

...the __integrity__ of it!

...the __genuineness__, and the __integrity__, and the __intensity__ of it!

You've got to accept, first of all, *the genuineness of God's love.*

That love he has for you *is for real!*

…it is real, amen!

Listen to me now, if you want to be *an effective minister of Jesus,*

…before you start to counsel someone who come to you with any kind of problem, *begin there!*

Begin with, the integrity of God's love!

We, as God's ministers, we've got to get people to the place where we can get that person *to agree with the truth,*

…where we can get that person *to see and accept* the *fact* that God loves them!

Our whole job as ministers of the New Covenant, of the New Testament, *is to show people the integrity of God's love!*

Only when they truly receive that *can they be released,*

…from resentment, from fear, from guilt;

…they can forgive and release themselves,

...they can forgive those who have sinned against them,

...they can take authority over the devil,

...*real authority!*

...and they can be *fully released!*

...whatever their problem might have been.

1John 4:18

"There is no fear in love, but perfect love casts out all fear!"

...*cast out!*

...*it casts out fear!*

*"...for fear has to do with **punishment."***

...and **punishment** has to do with the breaking of the law.

...that **punishment** has to do with **guilt.**

...that **punishment** has to do with **condemnation.**

...that **punishment** has to do with **suffering** guilt,

...**suffering** under condemnation,

*…**suffering under** the father of lies and deception,*

*…**suffering by the hand of** the accuser of the brethren.*

*…**and God doesn't want any of that!***

*…**God doesn't want any of us, any of His kids, suffering, being punished, tormented; suffering torment by of any of these things!***

God wants to destroy him who has the power of death in your life!

He wants to destroy him who has the power *of that death,* which is the devil; the accuser of the brethren; the father of *lies and darkness and confusion and deception!*

Hebrews 2:15

"…and deliver those who through fear of death…"

(…through the torment of that death; through the fear that it instills; the fear of judgment and of punishment)

God wants to, *and has delivered,*

"…those who through that fear and torment of death were subject to lifelong bondage"

You see **the salvation of Jesus Christ sets us free from two things:**

It sets us free from a _sin-consciousness;_

…from a _guilt-complex;_

…_from a constant focus and awareness of sin and guilt and the inferiority it brings, and the unworthiness!_

And it sets us free from _the power of sin;_

…from _the dominion of death;_

…it sets us free _from that death!_

It is so acutely crucial, so vital, that we understand and believe that, whom the Son sets free, is free indeed!

We must understand and also believe it in full, amen,

…_so we can fully enter into the reign of righteousness!_

You see in this book, and in our church, and in our discipleship school, _I am emphasizing the breaking and destroying of the dominion of death,_

…so that God can establish in people's hearts and lives,

…and in <u>your</u> heart and life,

…the <u>reign</u> of righteousness!

Chapter 10

Jesus defeated sin in the flesh!

God wants to open our eyes, *so that we can see how this righteousness reigns,*

…so that we can discover, how does it operate, *practically, in our very lives?*

…so that we can know, *how can I yield to it?*

…so that I can reign over death, and over the fear of death;

…over that whole thing of sin and death and what it brings and produces in my life!

Let's get back to Romans 8:3 now.

Romans 8:3,

*"**For God has done**, what the Law, weakened by the flesh, could not do, sending His Son, in the likeness of sinful flesh, and as an offering for sin. **He condemned sin in the flesh**!"*

1Peter 1:3 says,

"Blessed be the God and Father of our Lord Jesus Christ;"

*"…By His great mercy **we have been born anew**,"*

*"…**to a living hope**,"*

*"…**by the resurrection of Jesus Christ** from the dead."*

Do you see that it is **the truth concerning the resurrection** that makes the new birth in your spirit possible?

It's by *believing that truth*, that new life; that a new lifestyle *is given birth to* in my spirit!

The resurrection makes the new birth possible!

The resurrection makes the new life possible!

The resurrection *makes that new lifestyle possible!*

Without the truth of the resurrection;

…**without the truth of what exactly happened there;**

…**without the truth of *our resurrection there in Him* …to newness of life,**

…**that new birth in us;**

…***that new life;***

...that new lifestyle is impossible!

Colossians 1:18 says,

*"He is the head of the body; the Church. **He is the beginning,**"*

"...the first born from the dead."

It's the resurrection that makes *the birth of that new reality and that new life* possible for all of us!

He is the beginning of what?

The beginning of the new creation!

He is the first born from the dead!

It is His resurrection *that gives us the release from that law of sin and death!*

You see it is not the baptism of the Holy Spirit that will release you from the law of sin and death; *it is the truth of the resurrection!*

The baptism of the Holy Spirit is to equip you for service,

...so you could minister even more effectively.

The baptism of the Holy Spirit has got nothing to do with this <u>release</u> from the law of sin and death.

…it's got nothing to do with your <u>release</u> from the law of sin and death, you see,

You got released from that law of sin and death *<u>in the resurrection</u> of Jesus Christ,*

…and <u>through that resurrection</u>,

…and you get released into it <u>through the truth</u>, *and through <u>the power</u> of the resurrection;*

…through that <u>birth of faith</u> in your spirit *and the <u>power</u> that comes to you <u>through revelation</u>,*

…you get released into it <u>through the birth of that new understanding</u> *and <u>through that new life</u> that <u>gets released</u> by it in your spirit!*

It all becomes mine, *through the renewing of the mind!*

As I discover what I am,

As I discover who I am!

As I discover myself in Christ Jesus!

It all becomes mine, when I finally _realize_ that, hey listen, _**I don't have to submit**_ to the lies of the devil any more;

...*there is **no more need*** for me to buy into his deception!

Chapter 11

The devil has no real power!

Before the cross of Jesus Christ, *Satan could legally exercise his dominion;*

...his strong influence over man, **through the law of sin and death**.

He could do it, *because he had the power to do it.*

But in the cross and in the resurrection and in the ascension *that power was taken away from Him!*

That power was destroyed!

That legally binding power was legally destroyed!

So now, *since the resurrection,* what power is the only power left for him to operate in now?

Ignorance and deception!

The only power left that the devil can operate in now is *ignorance and deception!*

Satan doesn't have any more legal power *to keep any person on planet earth in bondage!*

That means: *He doesn't have any* <u>*real*</u> *power!*

He doesn't have any <u>real</u> power *to keep any person on planet earth in bondage!*

Not anymore!

Satan does not have <u>any</u> <u>more</u> <u>power</u> <u>left</u> to keep anyone in bondage *except for ignorance and deception!*

He doesn't have <u>any</u> power, *but through deception and through ignorance.*

That's why we must proclaim the truth!

We must *shout it from the rooftops,*

...and through modern media devices,

...and through whatever means possible,

...*so we may get the world's attention!*

This is exactly why the Scriptures say that we must PREACH; we must BOLDLY PROCLAIM, in BOLD CONFIDENCE,

...we must LIFT UP OUR VOICE IN STRENGTH,

…in BOLD CONFIDENCE,

…and PREACH the gospel,

…preach THE TRUTH,

…proclaim THE GOOD NEWS,

…TO EVERY CREATURE,

…to EVERY PERSON,

…EVERYWHERE on planet Earth!

…even if they travel or scatter to the far reaches of the universe itself!

We must find them and tell them the GOOD NEWS!

Hallelujah!

You see, when we share with them the gospel of Jesus Christ, *the truth* of His salvation; *the truth* of *their* redemption,

*…those chains of **deception** just melt, you see,*

…it's a prison with paper walls!

…and they will discover as you share with them,

'Hey, I too can walk free! I can live free!'

101

…because the gospel comes and sticks its finger right through that paper wall *and reveals the truth;*

…**it exposes the lie <u>*and reveals the truth,*</u>**

…**and destroys that *paper stronghold* of ignorance and deception!**

Listen, only through **the curse,**

…only through **the fall and its consequences,**

…could the devil **operate** his power,

…and exercise his **control;**

…and **operate** in sickness and disease and poverty and death,

…and he could exercise his **authority,**

…and just keep people **in bondage,**

…and hold whole nations **in bondage.**

And listen, even now, many many nations and many many people **are in bondage!**

Why?

Why are they still **in bondage?**

Not because Jesus *hasn't died!*

Not because Jesus *isn't alive!*

Not because Jesus *hasn't risen from the dead!*

BUT BECAUSE the Church is not doing their job right!

…**BECAUSE** the Church **is not preaching <u>the truth</u>!**

…**BECAUSE** the Church is *also* **deceived!**

The Church has been taken captive by this false man-made religious thing we call Christianity,

…it is full of man-made customs and traditions,

…and man-made philosophies,

…it is full of lies and deception and man-made doctrines,

*…**deceptive doctrines of demons!***

That's the only possible reason why people at large **are still in bondage** today!

…because we have <u>deceived ourselves</u>!

…we have come to the <u>wrong conclusions</u> in the gospel!

…we have forsaken <u>the truth</u> of the gospel!

...we have twisted <u>the truth</u> of the gospel!

*...thus, we are **believing a lie**,*

*...preaching a, **watered down, compromised,** gospel,*

...and <u>not</u> doing our job!

True Christianity <u>is defined by God</u>, not man!

And, *"Church"* is not something we <u>do</u>; *it's <u>who we are</u>!*

We don't <u>go</u> to Church; *we <u>are</u> the Church!*

And I'm not saying that we don't need buildings and that we now need to neglect meeting together.

We are not just the Church individually, *but we are part of the Church corporately!*

We are the family and household of God!

And we need to be <u>knitted together</u> and <u>welded together</u> by the <u>abiding word</u>,

...being strengthened by <u>the truth</u> of the gospel, and strengthening one another in <u>the truth</u>, every time we get together,

...so that we can be encouraged <u>together</u> and <u>pull together</u>,

...to begin to <u>focus our energy</u> and <u>resources</u> <u>together</u> on promoting <u>the truth</u> of the gospel,

...and getting the whole world <u>to see it</u> and <u>believe it</u>; to <u>embrace</u> it,

...because it is <u>the truth</u> of <u>their</u> identity;

...<u>the truth</u> of who <u>they</u> are!

They are God's very own dear children, *<u>whom He loves</u>!*

...and He wants to see them, <u>totally</u> <u>reconciled</u> to Him!

...He wants to see them, <u>restored</u> to their <u>true identity</u> and <u>original design</u>!

...living an adventurous, victorious, rich, fulfilled Christian life!

...full of love and friendship and LIFE!

Listen, God is not interested in *mere religious obedience and submission.*

God is love, and He longs to have an <u>intimate love relationship</u> with <u>you</u>, and <u>me</u>, and <u>every single individual</u> on this planet!

This is what differentiates Christianity from all other religions.

Every religion, *even the so called Christian religion, not the real thing, the man-made religion,* is governed by a system of moral codes, rules and laws.

True Christianity, on the other hand, *has nothing to do with that!*

True Christianity is not a religion!

True Christianity is <u>a faith relationship</u> with the God of all truth!

True Christianity is <u>a love relationship</u> with the living God, <u>our true Father</u>!

Religion as a whole *represents mankind's ignorance about their <u>true origin</u> and <u>identity</u>!*

What was the mission of Jesus Christ; the Messiah?

The Son of God was not sent to start the Christian religion!

He did not come to win a few protest votes against Moses, Mohammed or Buddha!

Jesus did not come to join forces with them either!

...to, you know, *<u>further condemn</u> the world.*

No!

He was sent to *free the world!*

He came to restore us back to our true origin and identity!

He came to reconcile us with our Father God!

After 4000 years of man's existence on this planet, and man-made religious guesses about God, **God, *having given all other alternatives enough time to fail,* and to be proven useless, finally *came in person, to set the record straight.***

In the fullness of time, *God sent forth His Son,*

…and so, when Jesus arrives on the scene, He says, **to all those who have lost their way, *and being deceived and lied to* by religion:**

"Come unto Me, all you who labor and are heavy laden…

(…with unnecessary and confusing man-made religious doctrines and burdens and customs and traditions),

"Come unto Me …and I will give you rest!"

"If anyone thirsts (after truth)*, let him come unto Me and drink, **and he shall never thirst again!"***

"I am the way (back to the Father)*, the truth and the life! No one can come unto the Father, except through Me,* (…**through understanding and believing and embracing My work of redemption**)*"*

*"**Everyone who believes** in Him, shall no longer perish, but **have, everlasting, eternal, abundant, life!**"*

*"**Everyone who believes** in Him passes from death to life! **And sin <u>no longer</u> has a hold on them!**"*

Jesus, the true light of the world, *that enlightens every man;* the Alpha and Omega; beginning and end of faith, *came!*

Truth Himself came!

*"The Law was given by Moses, **BUT grace and truth came** (in person) **through Jesus Christ!**"*

Grace came in person!

Life Himself came in person!

Truth came in person!

It was Jesus Christ!

God was in Christ, reconciling the world to Himself!

He came to reconcile the world back to Himself;

...not to hold their trespasses against them!

He came to reconcile the world to Himself;

...not to Judge them and condemn them!

Jesus came as Savior of the world!

Jesus came to bring us back to God's original thought;

...that romance of the ages,

...that He had in mind from the beginning!

He came to reveal a relationship that exists between God and man *that is larger than the fall!*

The 'LOGOS' that became flesh *revealed us; our true design and identity and purpose!*

You see, Jesus Christ came and *justified the Father's design of the human being!*

He came to prove that we belong to the Father, and not the devil!

He came to prove God's love for us, His kids!

He came to reveal and restore that love relationship in all its glory, <u>to the fullest</u>!

In Him the blueprint of our lives has been revealed, and our true design, <u>the truth</u> about our identity, is on display, there in Him.

Because of the cross, the sin transaction; the transaction by which we became slaves to sin, *was cancelled!*

Religious ignorance continues to make much of the fall,

...and continues to belittle the successful work of Jesus Christ's redemption and restoration of the human race!

But listen; there is no use for us to say:

'God, just please do something about it!'

'God, just please save the world!'

<u>God has done it</u>!

It is time for the Church to wake up!

...and to rise up!

...and to begin to shine!

...and to PROCLAIM!

*…*the REAL GOSPEL!

*…*the <u>TRUTH</u> OF THAT GOSPEL!

It is time for the Church to move,

…in the revelation, and the power <u>of this truth</u>!

*…*revealed so clearly in this book,

…and revealed so clearly, and so strong and convincingly, in the Scriptures themselves also!

But before I get carried away here, and get beside myself, let's continue there in Romans 8:3.

Chapter 12

The Fall was totally cancelled in Jesus!

Jesus came in the likeness of sinful flesh,

…**and He condemned sin in the flesh!**

Can you see now, more clearly, exactly what happened when Jesus came and condemned sin in the flesh?

He **fully partook** of flesh and blood!

He **fully partook** of death!

He **took the full blow** of the curse **upon Himself!**

…**the complete blow;**

…**the complete punishment of man!**

He took the whole Fall upon Himself!

…**the fullness of it!**

He took Sin upon Himself!

The complete punishment of man, *that death, He took upon Himself!*

He took the complete punishment of man *when He was made sin for us and became Sin,*

...*and became the One who represents Sin,*

...*and represents that whole fall, the fullness of it, in His person!*

The truth is: He did that; *He took all of it upon Himself!*

...so that He might enter into that realm of death,

...its domain,

...its kingdom,

...the very stronghold of its domain,

...the very stronghold of the devil!

Through fear of death, *the devil and his demonic forces reigned!*

They knew, *'Man, we have this whole world just where we want it!'*

I mean, every person knows they are going to have to die one day, *and that fear controls them!*

Why?

Because you see, **they are already dead spiritually!**

There are two deaths talked about in the Scriptures:

Spiritual death,

…and the death of the body.

I want you to see something truly intriguing here:

Isaiah 53:9 says,

Talking about Jesus…

"And they made His grave with the wicked and with the rich man in His death"

The Hebrew word used there for *"death"* is **plural**:

*"And they made His grave with the wicked and with the rich man in His …**deaths**"*

Do you see that **Jesus had to represent both deaths!**

He had to partake of **both**,

…**spiritual separation from God!**

...and physical separation from life!

He had to <u>partake</u> of that separation from life itself!

...from Life Himself!

...*in order to <u>fully represent</u> us!*

...*in order to <u>fully represent</u> the death of that death we were partakers of!*

...*in order to <u>fully represent</u> the end of the fall and all its consequences!*

I want you to see this clearly, that,

...if Jesus did not take on our sin <u>*and represented it*</u> in His physical body,

...<u>*and represented it*</u> in Himself personally,

...He would perhaps still be hanging on that cross!

...I mean, He would not have died physically *because <u>He would not have partaken</u> of death spiritually!*

And this is just a theory. The Bible does not say this directly anywhere, *but I think it is implied,* so don't stone me now,

...*but, <u>He partook</u> of our spiritual death,*

...He partook of our separation from God!

...and His physical death followed!

So, Jesus had to fully represent our sin; Sin itself, in order to partake of death,

...and in the same way He had to fully partake of flesh and blood, in order to fully partake of physical death as well!

Thus, He had to partake of two things in order to die twice:

He had to become sin; He had to be made sin; *He had to represent Sin itself in His own person,* in order to partake of our separation from God, and our separation from that eternal life we were made for,

...the life of our original design and true identity as children of God.

He joined us in that separation, and He partook of it fully, and He cried out in agony on that cross,

"My God! My God! Why have you forsaken Me!"

Can you imagine that?

Hey that's love!

He even partook of our forsakenness!

...our feelings of forsakenness!

God came in person, to answer fallen humanities cry of pain and deception and lies, and feelings of God-forsakenness,

...and He demonstrated on that cross the TRUTH,

...the truth that He has never forsaken us!

He has never forsaken us, in spite of the fall!

He still loves us!

...and He has come to redeem us by that love and restore us to glory!

...to our original glory!

...to our original design!

...to our true identity!

...to our Daddy!

...to His intimate embrace!

...and to His personal intimate friendship!

...to personal intimate fellowship with Him!

He personally partook of our spiritual death, and then He died physically when

that water and blood flowed mingled from His side; from His body!

Chapter 13

Death got swallowed up by life!

So in His *deaths* He was buried,

…but He could not be held by death!

…because of the power of that act of righteousness!

…because of the holiness of such love demonstrated!

He could not be held!

Tremendous power was released from Heaven in one legal act!

…because of a legal declaration!

…declaring the end of the fall!

…declaring man's total release!

Acts 2:24 says,

"…but God raised Him up…"

(Jesus, yes; **but us included also,** amen!)

"…God raised Him (and **us**) *up **having loosed the pangs*** (or the snare) ***of death**,"*

*"…**because it was not possible for Him*** (or for us) ***to be held by it!**"*

*…***it was not possible for Him**, *and therefore also for us,* **to be held by it!**

Hallelujah!

He loosed the snare of death!

Romans 4:25 also says to us, that,

*"**He was delivered up; given over to death, because of our sins, and then He was raised, <u>because of our justification</u>;**"*

*"…**because we were made righteous and declared righteous!**"*

*"…**because we were made innocent and declared innocent!**"*

Hallelujah!

In His death, *we died!*

And in His resurrection, *we were raised to newness of life!*

Ha… ha… ha… can you just imagine how glad the devil and his demons were when they had Him in the grave and when He went down into

Hades, into the place of the dead, into the lover parts!

The Bible says He descended into the lower parts of the earth (Ephesians 4:9)

(Note: Romans 10 also says:

"The word of faith which we preach does not say: 'Who will descend into the lower parts of the earth; into the deep; into the abyss, that is to bring Christ back from the dead'")

…Jesus descended into Hades; into the lower parts; into the deep abyss; into darkness,

…and the devils were rejoicing in triumph!

…and thinking: *'We've got Him, we've got Him, we've got Him! We've got Him now, the Son of God, we've got Him! We have the son of man; we have the Son of God right in our grip!'*

…and they tried to put those pangs; that snare of death, right around Him also,

…and tie Him down with it, *just like they do us;*

…and lock Him down there in that place forever.

But then suddenly!

Out of the legal courts of Heaven itself,

...Love Himself lifted up His voice and declared:

'It's enough!'

'It's more than enough!!'

And that same Spirit of God,

...that same Spirit of life itself,

...that resurrection Spirit,

...full of the power of life itself,

...full of the 'ZOE' or LIFE of God...

The Spirit of God raised Jesus Christ up from the dead!

And He loosed those pangs; that snare!

And that declaration from the Father,

...that Law of the Spirit of Life,

...legally <u>raised us up together</u> with Jesus!

We were literally <u>*raised to newness of life*</u> together with Jesus!

We were literally seated with Him *in that same place of authority and reign and dominion* in the heavenly places;

...in the heavenly realm;

...in the spirit realm,

...in that unseen realm of spirit realities!

...in that spirit dimension of <u>real spiritual authority</u>!

Can you just imagine with me,

Here was Jesus, and He further emptied Himself,

He totally emptied Himself!

He literally emptied Himself!

...to where He was as weak as weak can be!

...to where He was every bit as weak as us!

...as weak as weak as anything...

...and he laid there in the pangs of death!

...totally paralyzed under the curse of death!

...totally paralyzed under the full impact of the fall and its curse!

He laid there under the full impact of that curse and He was paralyzed!

He was helpless!

Can you just imagine!

I mean, this was the Son of God Himself!

The mighty Son of God!

The One who said to the wind:

"Be still!"

And it obeyed Him!

The One who spoke to disease:

"Be gone!"

And it went!

The One who said to demons:

"Come out!"

And they went out!

And here He was, and He was paralyzed, lying there in the grips of death!

And suddenly!

Because of God's decree!

Suddenly, that Spirit of God, full of resurrection life, touched Him!

And those strong chains of death, just snapped!

Death itself was broken!

He partook of death, *to destroy him who had the power of death!*

And He said:

'*Thank you very much, devil!'*

And He took the keys of death and of hell and of the grave and He rose victorious!

Hallelujah!

Ha… ha… ha… and the devil was still standing there, wondering what just happened?

…and while he was still standing there, bewildered,

Jesus stripped him of his authority!

He stripped him naked!

He stripped him of the supposed legality of the fall that he was hiding behind!

And He left him exposed and embarrassed!

The devil had nothing left when Jesus was done with him!

And then Jesus took those keys and unlocked every prison gate in that realm of death!

And He released us all!

And He raised us up in triumph together with Him!

He raised us up to newness of life!

Chapter 14

To each and every one of us grace was given!

And now Ephesians 4:7 says:

*"…**and to each one of us grace was given**,"*

*"…**according to the measure of Christ's gift**"*

(…**His gift of redemption**)

"This is then why it is also written:

'When He ascended on High, He led captivity captive…'

(Or a better translation would be: *"He led the captives **out!**"* **He led us out in His triumph, in His train of freedom!**)

'…and He gave gifts to men'

(Or: *"**He gave this as a gift to men**"*

He gave this salvation as a gift to men, *to mankind!*)

Another translation says:

*"He gave men gifts **to proclaim His triumph**"*

(…to proclaim these things;

…to proclaim the gospel of our salvation!

*…**to proclaim the work of redemption!***

*…**to proclaim that good news!***)

Hey, that works for me too! Amen!

It means that He then also gave gifts to men, *to proclaim this gift;*

…to proclaim this salvation, *as a gift already given!*

…it was given in love!

…it was given free of charge!

…it was given to all men! Amen!

Jesus triumphed over the government of sin and death, *and <u>released</u> the law of the Spirit of life, <u>to operate in the lives of all those who would dare believe</u> what He did, and <u>embrace fully</u>, that gift of salvation and redemption and restoration and righteousness!*

Do you now see what is behind our faith?

We are not merely believing in some cleverly devised man-made myth;

…some fable!

…some cleverly devised little doctrine of men and of demons!

…some pretty little made up nonsensical story and lie!

No!

We are living in the power of His resurrection!

The government of the life of the Spirit is established in the power of the resurrection of Jesus Christ!

That government; *that life of the Spirit is real*!

And it is established, in that resurrection!

…in that power released there!

That resurrection life is the most powerful life that we can ever partake of!

Chapter 15

Jesus gave sin a death blow!

Jesus Christ condemned sin in the flesh!

…He defeated sin in the flesh!

…He gave it a death blow!

Let's go back there to Romans 8

Romans 8:1

"There is <u>therefore</u> now no condemnation for those who are in Christ Jesus!"

Do you now see in what context it was actually written?

This gospel of truth is so far above that other weak and inferior gospel interpretation!

Romans 1:16

"I am not ashamed of this gospel!" Paul says,

"It is the power of God unto salvation!"

"...for everyone who believes!"

God's gospel is so much better than man's gospel!

I don't even know how people could for so long, for so many years, interpret the gospel in such a weak misguided way, with such an inferior interpretation!

What shall we say to this gospel of truth?

Romans 6:1

"What shall we say?"

"Shall we continue in sin that grace may hopefully continue to abound?"

"By no means!"

...you flaky thing you!

...ha... ha... ha...

No! God forbid!

Hallelujah!

Romans 8:1

"There is <u>therefore</u> <u>now</u> no condemnation for those who are in Christ Jesus!"

Verse 2,

"For the Law of the Spirit of Life, in Christ Jesus, (that work of redemption; that declaration,) *has set me free from the law of sin and death!"*

We can also read it this way:

"For the spirit law of life, (that resurrection life released to me in Christ Jesus) *has set me free from the law of sin and death!"*

Here is another way of reading it also,

"For the law of the spirit, life in Christ Jesus (the law of faith; the faith life; believing the truth of the gospel; living life as a Christian; living the Christ-life) *has set me free from the law of sin and death!"*

Verse 3,

"For God has done, what the Law, weakened by the flesh, could not do, sending His Son in the likeness of sinful flesh, and as an offering for sin. He condemned sin in the flesh!"

"…in order that the just requirement of the Law might be fulfilled in us!"

Now notice how powerful this is.

What God has to say through our precious brother Paul here in verse 4 **is so powerful!**

"He condemned sin in the flesh!"

Not to establish victory for Himself!

No!

"He condemned sin in the flesh, in order that the just requirement of the Law might be fulfilled in us!"

"He was wounded for our transgressions; the chastisement that brought us peace was upon Him!"

"...in order that the just requirement of the Law might be fulfilled in us!"

What was the just requirement of the Law?

The soul that sins shall die!

The Law required that,

...**and you couldn't get away from it!**

If you sin, then, according to the Law of Moses, you were just in death, that's it!

The wages of sin is death!

"For all have sinned and fallen short of the glory of God, but the gift of God, in Christ Jesus, is eternal life!"

*"**He condemned sin in the flesh in order that the just requirement of the Law might be fulfilled in us who walk according to the Spirit** (...who walk according to the truth of redemption; according to faith, according to resurrection life and power; according to our new identity and spirit life; our true spirit identity; our restored spirit identity and new life) **and not according to the flesh!**"*

Listen, you can associate yourself with being a Christian, and even be part of a local Church body of believers, *the whole works,*

...**but if your mind is still <u>set</u> on carnal things; *<u>on your natural identity</u>* in the flesh, *you are walking according to the flesh!***

*...**and not according to the Spirit!***

*...**not according to <u>the truth</u>!***

...**and your mind will still continue to play tricks on you,**

*...**and you will remain mixed up in sin,***

...**and the devil has you right where he wants you!**

Walking this way, **with a mind still <u>set</u> on your natural identity;**

...**with a mind still <u>set</u>** on carnal things;

…on the strong but rather empty passions and desires of the flesh,

…with their mind still <u>set</u> on these things, *they found themselves **still trapped** in sin,*

…and so they thought,

'Now how is it possible for a Christian, supposedly born again, and saved, how is it that that Christian, that we then, still continue to sin?'

…and so, **based on their own experience of failure and defeat,** they inevitably began to interpret Romans 7 wrong,

…and they thought,

'Oh well, maybe that's just a general spiritual rule the Christian has to accept and understand and live by'

'Maybe it is just supposed to be like that!'

So, okay, let's face it, all of us, even you who are reading this book,

…let's face it, *even after being born anew of the truth,*

…*even after being saved, by coming to the knowledge of the truth,*

…even after coming to the full knowledge of the truth,

…we have all blown it and sinned since then,

…let's face that fact, we might as well,

…because it is true that sometimes *we fail to fully express who we really are,*

…we fail to express that new creation we truly are,

…and we blow it, and we sin, for a moment,

…but when we recognize that we are in error, that exact instant, we recognize it and notice it,

…we immediately snap out of it, *and get back to the truth, and the full expression of who we are, as new creations and children of God; partakers of the Divine nature; partakers of love in its purity!*

So, yes, we sometimes blow it, and we sin, *and we fail to fully live out our original design, and we sometimes fail to give a consistent full expression of our true identity as children of God,*

...but listen, **let's not make a rule of that!**

We don't have to stay weak, and just continue to fail, and sin,

139

...and live in the flesh ...in our minds, trapped, in an inferior identity!

We don't have to stay weak, and just continue to fail, and sin, *living like mere men!*

...trapped in an inferior expression of who we really are!

1John 2:1

"My little children, I write **this** *to you,* **so that you may not sin***"*

"...and **if** *(not when, but* **if***) anyone does sin, we have an advocate who is in Heaven, with the Father"*

...He is one with the Father!

*...***and together they are still proclaiming** *the legal reality of your redemption,*

*...***and the truth of who you are, because of that work of redemption!**

They are still, together, *proclaiming your innocence by the blood of the New Testament!*

*...***and they want you to continue** *to* <u>*see*</u> *the truth, and* <u>*believe*</u> *the truth!*

…and as you begin to <u>genuinely *see yourself*</u>, *according to <u>the truth of the gospel</u>*,

…and continue to see yourself that way,

…<u>seeing yourself</u> as that innocent creature *who is partaking of a pure and innocent nature,*

…continuing <u>to see yourself that way</u>,

…your mind will be renewed, and you will be transformed *in the expression of who you are!*

…because you will <u>see</u> yourself differently!

…and <u>believe</u> yourself to be a different person!

…and you will actually begin to consistently *BE that new creature!*

…and live like that new creature!

…and walk like that new creature!

So, don't go dig a hole when you do blow it!

…and go and climb into it and condemn yourself, *and bury yourself under all that,*

…and flog yourself for it, and kill yourself with it! No! Grab a hold of the rope of truth and get yourself out of that hole.

…**because you have an advocate with the Father,** *and* <u>*He is God's own propitiation for our sins*</u>*, and not just for ours, but really, He is God's propitiation for the sins of the whole world!*

…**because the Father** <u>**sent Him**</u>**,**

…*and the two of them are* <u>*in total agreement*</u>*, concerning that legal release!*

…*and therefore also concerning* <u>*your true identity*</u>*, and* <u>*your innocence*</u>*!*

You are God's workmanship, created there in Christ Jesus, in that work of redemption!

…*you were reconciled to them there, at great personal cost to them!*

…**and they love you!**

…*because they are your origin!*

…*because you are God's child!*

…*children of God!*

But Paul says here in Romans 8:4 that, **hey listen, we may now walk after the Spirit;**

142

...after our true spirit identity;

...after the truth of what happened to us, in the spirit realm, in that work of redemption!

...he says **we <u>may now</u> walk after the Spirit,**

...and not after the flesh!

We <u>need not</u> walk after the flesh anymore!

We <u>need not be</u> dictated to by the lusts of the flesh!

Chapter 16

The lusts of the flesh

What do the lusts *of "the flesh"* refer to?

I mean what does that term *"the flesh"* refer to?

Our bodies, yes,

…but more accurately, that term, *"the flesh,"* refers to **that old mindset**,

…**the law of sin and death governing our thinking and our actions!**

We <u>need not be</u> dictated to by that old Fall-mindset!

We <u>need not be</u> dictated to by that old sin-mentality!

We <u>need not be</u> dictated to by that old sin and death system!

We <u>need not be</u> dictated to by that old law of sin and death anymore!

Paul says,

Romans 8:5,

"They that walk after the flesh, are the ones who <u>set their minds</u>, on the things of the flesh!"

That means, if you sit around as a mere natural-minded man, and think about fleshly things all the time, then you might as well know it, *<u>the flesh</u>; that natural identity, is still going to dominate you!*

...that worldly natural-identity-minded sin-*mentality* ...the lust of the eyes, the lust of the flesh, and the pride of life *is still going to rule you!*

...you will remain trapped in a natural-minded identity,

...*and in the flesh, <u>and in sin</u>!*

...*the flesh is still going to dominate you!*

It has no right to!

God's done everything He could possibly do, as God, to break the dominion of that thing over your life!

But if you willfully go and let your mind dwell on those things, you might as well know it; *the flesh will still dominate you,*

...*and you will still involve yourself with sin,*

…and the law of sin and death will continue to operate in your life again!

Romans 8:5,

"Those who live according to the flesh…"

You see, we still live in this body, and this body is still flesh and blood,

…so you and I are still partaking of flesh and blood, amen,

I mean, **we are not partaking of a glorified body yet.**

And this flesh and blood body we are partaking of can still easily partake of and commit *every possible sin in the book,*

*…***whether you are a Christian or not!**

This flesh and blood body we are partaking of can still partake of and commit *every sin that it could commit before the birth of faith in your heart;*

I mean it can still just as easily partake of and commit *every sin from before you became a Christian!*

*…**every sin** from before!*

It is possible for this flesh body, and for this mind of ours, to become occupied in every possible sin!

BUT ONLY IF YOU LET IT!

Romans 6 tell us clearly that, **God has placed us back into government of our own lives again!**

Romans 6:12 says,

"Let not sin therefore, reign in your flesh and blood bodies, to make you obey its passions!"

Verse 13 says,

"Do not yield your members to sin, as instruments of sin!"

Verse 14 says,

"For sin shall not have dominion over you!"

And then again in verse 16, he emphasizes it again,

He says,

"Do you not know?"

In other words, **you should know,**

…but many don't!

He says,

"Do you not know that if you yield yourselves to anyone, as an obedient slave,

…you are that one's slave whom you choose to obey?"

…you are that things SLAVE!

…that very thing you choose to yield to!

…you are its SLAVE, that which you choose to obey!

YOU ARE A SLAVE!

You are no better than a SLAVE!

"…either of sin, which leads to death,

…or of righteousness, which leads to consistent freedom and life!

Consistent expression of that righteousness,

…that consistency in the expression of Righteousness is what defines holiness!"

I want you to notice that it is **faith in the righteousness given to me in redemption;**

…yielding to that faith and that righteousness,

…it is that practical *faith-reality,*

…that <u>faith</u> that overcomes the world;

…*it is that <u>faith</u> that defines holiness!*

That kind of <u>faith</u> expression, that very *faith-life* is the very definition of holiness!

So, you see, it is possible to fall again and partake of every sin,

…*but only if you let it happen!*

God has placed you back into government again!

You see, we as the Church of Jesus, are going to have to start discovering *the reign of righteousness* if we are ever going to live in victory!

Because that reign of righteousness in your mind is what gives you the authority and the ability to reign!

It introduces to you the working of God within you!

…*both to will and to do according to His good pleasure!*

But you see *that truth of the gospel;*

...that truth of your original design and true identity as child of God restored to you in redemption;

...that reign of righteousness,

...must be submitted to if you and I are ever going to live in victory!

If we don't yield to it...

...if I don't yield to it, and I prefer, to just continue ignorantly,

...then listen man, *the devil is going to take advantage!*

...he is going to take *FULL advantage,* like he has so often in the past!

...like he has done to so many precious Christians,

...and just trap them back into sin again!

Chapter 17

Your mind is the key to victory!

IT HAPPENS IN THE MIND!

Setting the mind again on the things of the flesh!

Do you see that the enemy wants to trip you up **in your thought-life?**

Paul continues to say there in Romans 6:19,

He says,

*"I am writing and speaking to you about these things, **because of your natural thinking;***

*…**because of a weakened understanding;***

*…**because you yield your thought-life to sin,***

*…**and then your members;***

*…**the flesh body you live in follows.***

*…**That's how the process happens!"***

He says there,

"For just as you once yielded your mind, and then your members, to impurity; to lies and deception and polluting of the truth about yourself; the truth of who you really are as child of God,"

He says,

"...so now, yield your members, to righteousness, for sanctification"

If we're just automatically immune to sin now, I wouldn't need to be wearing an armor *made up of the truth of the gospel; the truth of the work of redemption,*

...I wouldn't need to worry about wearing that armor; about fighting off temptation now would I?

What makes temptation, **temptation**?

The fact that, *should you yield to it, it becomes strong enough to get you!*

Temptation wouldn't be **temptation** if it wasn't possible for you to fall for it and yield to it!

Temptation wouldn't be **temptation,** *if it wasn't possible for it to grow in strength,* and for you to then yield to it!

Temptation wouldn't be **temptation** if it wasn't possible for you to fall for it and yield to it!

Would you agree with me?

You see if we were dealing with *sinless perfection* in the gospel;

...if it was *impossible for the Christian to sin,*

...we wouldn't even be talking about a temptation factor!

How many of you reading this book right now have been tempted, and have had the opportunity to sin, after you became a Christian?

...after you've been so called *"born again"* even?

...after you've come to know the truth?

...even after knowing the grace message?

...even after fully knowing these same redemption truths I preach and teach and write about?

The truth is,

...we have all been tempted, and have all had the opportunity to sin,

...even after,

...and dare I say,

...especially after God's truth and faith was birthed in our hearts, in our spirits, and have given birth to the new creation in our hearts and lives!

We might as well recognize that fact, **and realize that we do have an enemy** *that would just love to trip us up and snare us with sin!*

How many of you have had the opportunity to get sick, since you were saved by coming to the knowledge of the truth as it is revealed in Jesus?

I mean even with understanding the truth about physical healing being included in the work of redemption,

...and that it is our inheritance,

...that healing is the children's bread!

...even with the clear understanding of that truth, *we have all had the opportunity to get sick!*

You see, let's face it, **even after being established even in redemption truths;**

...in new creation *realities,*

...we still have those opportunities!

You might even face the opportunity to have every possible curse to come upon you!

…you'll have those opportunities in life!

…because the devil, <u>like</u> a roaring lion, <u>like</u> a hungry lion, *prowls around, seeking whom he may devour!*

"BUT," the Scriptures go on to say:

"…whom <u>resist</u>, steadfast in your faith!"

"…whom resist!"

<u>*…not tolerate!*</u>

"…whom <u>resist!</u>"

"<u>…steadfast in the faith!</u>"

"…putting him to flight in your life!"

Romans 8:5

"For those who live according to the flesh, <u>set their minds</u> on the things of the flesh…"

"…<u>BUT</u> those who live according to the Spirit, <u>set their minds</u> on the things of the Spirit (on spirit truth!)*"*

This is the very key to victory!

You are going to have to start studying *the importance of* **the renewing of the mind,**

...before you can ever truly live in victory!

You have to reprogram your computer brain, *your mind,* **with the word of God,**

...but not just any old kind of doctrine, and age old religious teaching!

No!

Your computer brain, *your mind, has to be wiped clean* **from all that shortsighted inaccurate and incomplete weak-minded teachings!**

Your computer brain, *your mind, has to be reprogrammed!*

Wiped clean and reprogrammed *with accurate New Testament, new creation, truth!*

Your mind has to be wiped clean and reprogrammed *with redemption realities!*

*...*with the mind of Christ!

Wiped clean and reprogrammed, *with the thoughts of God!*

With the truth about your identity and design and sonship! Amen!

If you want your Christianity to work for you,

...you've got to get fanatical about the truth of the gospel!

You've got to realize and recognize that,

'Hey, what happened in redemption and in the resurrection <u>is a reality</u>, not some myth or theory;

...<u>it's reality!</u>'

Amen!

...and it has everything to do with me!

It has everything to do with you!

You've got to mean business *with these truths; with these realities!*

And you've got to become fanatical with it!

...so you can get serious with God!

...so that what you have between you and God is real faith!

...so that what you have in fellowship and relationship with God <u>is truly real</u>!

...and it's based on truth; <u>on reality</u>!

...*it is based on the "Word of Truth,"*

...*the accurate gospel of your salvation and redemption and restoration to glory!*

...*being one with the Father and with Jesus and with the indwelling Holy Spirit!*

...*and living and walking in that glory!*

...*living and moving and having your being in God!*

You are going to have to get fanatical *if you want your Christian faith to be real and powerful!*

If you want your Christianity to work for you!

You are going to have to get fanatical *with the truth!*

With the thoughts of God!

With the mind of Christ!

Until, through the truth, *you get that law of faith and that law of the Spirit <u>activated</u> on the inside of you, and you have that resurrection power <u>flowing</u> on the inside of you!*

...and you wake up in the morning, *thinking truth,*

...thinking Jesus!

Until you go to bed at night, *thinking redemption realities,*

...and thinking Jesus!

Waking up in the middle of the night even, *thinking precious Father God and Holy Spirit thoughts!*

Enjoying those *New Testament Scriptures!*

Enjoying that *eternal life!*

Enjoying *faith thinking!*

Enjoying *apostolic thinking!*

Pure gospel thoughts!

Full of love and worth and value and identity and belonging!

Experiencing *the embrace* of the Father!

*...*of your Daddy God!

Experiencing His *nearness!*

Dreaming about His *truth,* in your spirit!

*...*and about *Him!* Amen!

Experiencing that *LIFE!*

And then you are going to start *speaking these things!*

Speaking Jesus!

Speaking pure anointing!

Speaking pure power!

Speaking life-changing radical stuff!

Giving voice to God's truth and to God's Spirit and to God's power!

…because out of the abundance of the heart the mouth cannot help but speak!

And you are going to *live it!*

You are going to *live and walk and talk Jesus and His redemption and Father God!*

You are going to *live and walk and talk Daddy God and all men's embrace in His bosom; in His heart of love!*

…and that resurrection LIFE <u>will just keep flowing</u> out of you!

…because you have <u>fully engaged and activated</u> that law of the Spirit of life in Christ Jesus!

…and it <u>sustains</u> your freedom and your very LIFE in Him!

Chapter 18

Sin-nature?

'Brother Rudi, all this sounds fabulous, and I'd very much like to believe these things, but it's all just too theological, and theoretical, I mean, **it is all just to good to be true, isn't it!**'

'Because, where does the sin-nature come in?'

'I mean, you make no room for it in your teaching!'

'So, how does the sin-nature factor in?'

'Because, I mean, Romans 7:25 says, "…so then, in myself, in my mind, I am a slave to God's Law, but in the sinful nature I am a slave to the law of sin"

Now listen I know your Bible says that, but listen very acutely carefully to me now.

You see, many of our translations,

…because of inaccurate theology, and wrong understanding, in the minds of the translators,

…many of our translations use the words, "sinful nature," or "sin-nature,"

…but it is nowhere to be found *in the original Scriptures;*

…*it is not in the Greek at all!*

There is no sinful-nature!

You can't have two natures!

You cannot plant pumpkin seeds, and have a peach tree, or a pecan tree, come up.

That pumpkin seed doesn't have two natures!

It doesn't have a little bit of pumpkin, and a little bit of mango, and a little bit of papaya!

Ha… ha… ha… *there is no such thing as a fruit-salad-seed!*

Luke 6:44 says:

*"**For men do not gather figs from thorns, nor do they gather grapes from a bramble bush!**"*

And James 3:11 & 12 says,

*"**Does a spring send forth fresh and bitter water from the same opening? Or can a fig tree, my brethren, bear olives, or a grapevine bear figs?**"*

No! Amen!

You see, in Romans 7 Paul was referring to a life experience under the Law.

He starts off and plainly says that he is now writing:

*"…**to those who know the Law**"*

(…those who are intimately acquainted with the Law)

Thus, he is not referring to his life in Christ, as a Christian;

…he is referring to his life and his experience under the Law!

But he is also writing it as a warning to all those who want to mix in the Law with their Christian Faith.

He essentially says that, it will not, and cannot work!

Introducing just a little bit of Law into Christianity *is like introducing just a little bit of leaven into a lump of dough.*

That little bit of leaven; *just a little bit of Law mixed in with your Christian faith, will leaven the whole lump!*

It will change and ruin your whole experience of Grace and Truth,

...and put you right back under the influence and power and government of the law of sin and death!

He makes it clear in Romans 6:14 that,

...sin shall not be your master as a Christian,

...because we are no longer under Law, but under (the power and governing influence of) *Grace!*

I want you to notice that Romans 7 is sandwiched in between Romans 6 and Romans 8.

That last verse of Romans 7 I quoted earlier, verse 25, it cannot be taken out of context!

It is merely *a conclusion of all that was said in Romans 7.*

A conclusion of *our life and our experience as we used to know it under the Law!*

But it is prefaced by the greater conclusion Paul came to, and clearly stated in the previous verse, verse 24, *and also in the beginning of that same verse, verse 25.*

He says,

Romans 7:24,

"What a wretched man that I am! (*…*under the Law; not as a Christian) *Who will deliver me* (*…*who will rescue me) *from this body of death?"*

Verse 25,

*"**Thanks be to God** (…it was done) **through Jesus Christ our Lord!**"*

"…so then…"

(*…*in conclusion, in other words, *this is what my life and experience was like under the Law.* **God delivered me from that life. And I don't want *you* to remain trapped in that kind of a life either. It was horrible!** This is what it was like:)

*"…I myself in my mind was **a slave** to God's Law…*

(*…*and everyone who tries to live under the Law will still find this to be true!

*In yourself, in your mind, you will find yourself to be **nothing but a slave** to God's Law!*)

*"…I am **a slave** to God's Law, in my mind, **but** in my members, **in my soul, and in my body, I am a slave to the law of sin.**"*

That was life under the Law, *but not anymore!* Praise God!

"Wretched man that I am who would deliver me from this body of death? **I thank God; He did it through Jesus Christ!***"*

Then Romans 8:1,

*"***Therefore** (*…because of this glorious ultimate conclusion; *because of this salvation and redemption God accomplished in Christ Jesus*)

*"***Therefore** **there is now no condemnation***..."*

Another translation says:

*"***There is <u>therefore</u> now no condemnation for those who are in Christ Jesus;***"*

*"…***because in Christ Jesus***"*

(*…*and through Him; *through His work of redemption;* through His death, His burial, resurrection and ascension, *and ours with Him,* amen,)

*"…***in Christ Jesus, the law of the Spirit of life, set me free, from the law of sin and death!***"*

You see in Romans 7 Paul was referring *to* **the problem with that whole Law system***;*

…he was referring to the problem of living under the Law.

There was a problem with the Law, *with living under the Law, <u>because there was a problem with my mind</u>!*

…because my mind knows "Thou shalt not!"

…and with my mind I'm trying to live the Law,

…but man, ***the power of sin is not broken yet in my mind, and in my life, <u>because faith isn't birthed yet</u>!***

…because God's <u>truth</u>; God's <u>ultimate truth hasn't dawned on me and liberated my mind yet</u>!

Listen man, if you have two natures inside of you, *then half of you will have to go to hell,*

…and only half of you will make it into Heaven…

Ha… ha… ha…

Or, *you'll have to go to Heaven and Hell at the same time,* amen!

And that, my friend, is going to be terribly difficult!

Amen!

Ha… ha… ha…

So, go ahead and change your translation wherever it uses that phrase *"sin-nature"* or *"sinful nature,"*

…you have God's permission on that,

…**because it is not in the Greek!** *Amen!*

Those who still talk that way don't know what they're talking about!

They have no clue about spirit truth,

…nor new creation realities!

There is no need to even try and argue with them over these things.

If they want to argue with you, *just refuse to argue,*

…and refer them to 2Corinthians 5:17 & 18,

…where that same Paul, *who wrote most of the New Testament,*

…and from whom we got the revelation of God's true gospel,

…he states abundantly clearly that,

…**you are a new creature in Christ Jesus!**

…which according to him means:

*"...**the old things have** (...past tense) **passed away,***

*"...**<u>behold</u>,*" *he says,*

*"...**all things have become new!***"

*"...**now all these things are of God***"

(...this whole work of redemption,

...and every good thing *that is already in us*

*...**and that is awakened in us by the truth of the gospel;***

*...**by the truth of what happened in redemption;***

...by that <u>faith</u> we have from Him)

*"...**all these things, are of God,***

*...**who <u>has</u> reconcil<u>ed</u> us to Himself,***

*...**and gave us this message, as a ministry to others,***

*...**so they too may freely enter in, and enjoy, the reality of that reconciliation!***"

(Note that I didn't quote it exactly, *and I didn't twist it's meaning either,* but I didn't quote it exactly *so you will be forced to go read it for yourself! Ha... ha... ha...*)

Listen, the language of Romans 7,

"...the good I want to do, I can't do,"

...**that's not the language of the new creation!**

...**it's not New Testament!**

...**it's not New Covenant language!**

No!

The language of Romans 7,

*"...the good I want to do, **I can't do**,"*

...**that language,**

...***is the language of the law of sin and death!***

It's not the language of *the law of the Spirit of life in Christ Jesus!*

Hey listen, <u>faith</u> doesn't talk that way, amen!

Faith says,

*"...**I can do all things through Christ Jesus who strengthens me!**"*

The new creature says,

"…I <u>can</u> do all things in Christ Jesus!"

The new creation doesn't look for any excuse to be sick or to be sinful!

The new creation says,

'I know what is mine in Christ Jesus,

…I know my rights!

…I <u>can</u> do all things!

…I am more than a conqueror, because of Him, and through Him, who loves me, and gave Himself for me!'

*…*More than a conqueror, amen!

Hey that's new creature language! Amen!

Hallelujah!

…and it's established in the fact of the resurrection life that I partake of now!

Chapter 19

Set your mind on the truth of redemption!

And how does that resurrection life of Jesus Christ become a practical reality in my life?

It has everything to do with the renewing of the mind!

…with the embracing of truth in my inner man!

You cannot begin to enjoy the practical side of righteousness, *without the renewing of the mind!*

…without the impartation of that <u>faith</u> which God's accurate redemption truth alone can bring!

You cannot consistently enjoy these things and walk in them, *without setting your mind on things that are <u>above</u>!*

…setting your mind on the truth of God;

…on the things that are of the Spirit!

*...**setting** the mind!*

*...**setting** it!*

*...**cementing it**!*

Setting **your mind is no big deal!**

Your mind is a servant!

The thing was created to serve you!

Your mind was given to you to serve you,

...and what you put into it, will serve you!

...it will either bless you, or curse you!

...but your mind was designed to bless you,
amen!

Can you see yourself right now, *can you just see yourself,* **just so full of God!**

Just so full of the word of redemption!

Just so full of the truth of God!

Just so full of the Word,

...that when you open your mouth to speak,
the Word comes out!

Redemption comes out!

God comes out!

"...out of the abundance of the heart, the mouth speaks!"

"...Let the Word of Christ dwell in you richly!"

Are you going to do that?

I know that, that is exactly what I am going to do!

I am going to keep building, and strengthening, and reinforcing my faith!

I am going to keep focusing on these things; *these truths; these realities,*

...until it is such a reality in my own spirit and in my life!

I want *the fullness* of these things!

And I know you do too, that's why you haven't put this book down yet!

And, if I may be so bold, *that is exactly why some of you might need to come to our discipleship school,*

...so you can just set some time aside to focus on these things; these truths; these eternal realities,

...and be thoroughly equipped in these things *and thoroughly equipped in your spirit,* amen!

Hey listen I don't have a hidden agenda man!

I want the Word to dwell in me richly, *and I want that same Word to dwell in you richly also!*

I don't have any other focus or agenda in life!

I want to continue to be consumed with this message!

I want to continue to be consumed and energized and motivated from within by its zeal and its fire and its passion;

...by the love of God!

And I want the same for you, *nothing less!*

Listen if you have truly heard this truth *and embraced it in your inner man,*

...then you are indebted!

"...Now we are indebted, not to the flesh..."

Listen I don't owe the flesh anything!

Nothing man, NOTHING!

I'm indebted to God, *to live after the spirit!*

And I'm indebted also to the world!

I owe them something!

I owe them this good news!

That's why I write books, and preach, and run a discipleship school, and pastor a church!

…so that I can arrest men's conscience, *in these truths!*

…and establish them, *in these things!*

…*and present them to God,* as chaste virgins!

…*in love with God!*

…*and present them pure and undefiled by the flesh, and by the world, and by religion, and by the devil!*

And now you too,

…if you have <u>truly heard</u> these same truths,

…and have <u>truly embraced</u> them in your heart,

…*then you too are now indebted to the world,*

179

...to get involved in the ministry of God; this ministry of reconciliation!

Listen you owe the world the good news!

Get involved somewhere, amen!

If not in our ministry, *then somewhere where they understand these things,*

...and are truly busy with this ministry to the world;

...this ministry of truth and reconciliation and discipleship <u>in these things</u> God has entrusted us all with!

Listen, people truly do need that environment and that fellowship and focus together with other believers, in the truth, because Paul says, and he makes it clear that,

"...to set your mind on the things of the flesh, is death!" – Romans 8:6

'Oh, but I like to think about my old things, that's why I don't like to hang around other Christians too much, and commit to a local church, to a local body of believers, because they confront me about my stuff, and I don't like it, I feel condemned!'

Go ahead, think about, and hand on to all that old stuff, all your old things, but it's death baby!

If you like death, go for it, **I can't change your mind then, none of us can, no believer can, not even God can then!**

Romans 8:6,

"...to set your mind on the things of the flesh, is death!"

"...but, to set your mind on the spirit, on your spirit-identity, on the things of the Spirit, is life and peace!"

What does that peace speak of?

Reconciliation with God!

Romans 5:1,

"Now we have peace with God through our Lord Jesus Christ!"

Another translation puts it this way,

"Therefore, being justified by faith, we have peace with God!"

You see, righteousness;

...that dominion of righteousness, is only established, in that peace!

...in that reconciled, intimate, love and trust and faith relationship with God!

The kingdom of God is not the sinful,
fleshly, party life;

...it's not the natural identity;

...it's not the natural life;

...it's not food and drink,

...and it's not an empty religious existence
either, full of boring religious rituals!

No!

The kingdom of God is righteousness, joy,
and peace!

*"...You, oh Lord, will keep him in perfect
peace, <u>whose mind is stayed on You</u>!"*

Hallelujah!

The work of righteousness, or better yet,
the fruit of righteousness, *is peace!*

That *"Word of Righteousness"* works peace!

Hallelujah!

Listen, peace is the most powerful
experience that any man can live in!

...not false peace, *but real peace!*

...that transparency that you know that you have in your spirit; <u>that innocence</u>!

...you don't feel even the smallest little amount guilty!

...you don't feel embarrassed!

...you don't feel ashamed!

...you don't feel condemned at all!

...and you don't feel like, *'Oh, I don't feel like I truly belong!'*

...but you feel peace,

...only peace, and joy!

Isaiah 32:17,

"The affect of righteousness will be, peace; the result of righteousness, quietness and tranquility forever!"

Trust forever!

Faith forever!

"...the memory of the righteous is blessed!"

Amen! Isn't that beautiful?

Thank you Holy Spirit!

Chapter 20

Don't deceive yourself!

Let's quickly look at Romans 8:7,

…and, I'm almost done!

Romans 8:7

*"…***for the mind that is set on the flesh is hostile to God. It does not submit to God's law. Indeed it cannot!***"*

I want you to see this clearly.

Which law is he speaking about now?

He is speaking about the law of the Spirit of life!

God's law is no longer the Law of Moses, *it's now the law of the Spirit of life;*

*…**it's the Spirit of life,* amen!**

Now listen to me, Jesus has risen from the dead, it's a historical fact!

It is recorded in history, and it is on record!

It cannot be denied and it cannot be ignored!

Jesus Christ is raised from the dead!

The result of that resurrection is the law of Spirit and Life!

The law of the Spirit of life was released there!

...the spirit law of LIFE was released there!

...LIFE was released there!

...that SPIRIT LAW was released there!

<u>BUT</u> if the mind is not renewed and set on the things of the Spirit;

...on those things; *on those truths; on those realities,*

...*then that law cannot govern your life!*

Romans 8:7 says,

"...the mind that is set on the flesh,

...it cannot submit to God's law;

...it <u>cannot</u> submit!"

While your mind is on the things of the flesh, on your natural identity only, *<u>it is</u>*

***impossible** for you to submit to God's law, to God's redemption truth and reality!*

*…**and if you <u>cannot</u> submit to God's law, to God's redemption truth and reality, in your heart and in your mind, <u>you will still walk after the flesh</u>!***

Listen you can go and study how Paul writes about these things to the believers,

He says,

"I write to you,

 *…**to no longer live as the gentiles do,***

*…**they live in the futility of their minds!"***

*"**They live their lives** …**being alienated from the life of God, in every practical sense of the word**"*

*"**Why?**"*

*"…**because of the hardening of their hearts,***

*…**because of a darkened understanding**,"* he says!

Why is he writing this?

Why is he saying these things to the Christians?

Because, they were Christians; they were believers, supposedly *"born again,"* __BUT__ *they were still living like the gentiles do,* __in__ __the same defilement and futility of mind and__ __spirit!__

He essentially says,

'Hey listen guys, while you live __just like the__ __world does__*, it only shows me one thing:* __Your mind is not SET on the things of the__ __spirit, on the things of your spirit-identity,__ __on the things God__*!'*

In 2Corinthians 7:1 he says,

"Since we have these great redemption truths, and this mighty thrilling experience of these realities implicated for our very lives by these redemption truths,

…let us purify ourselves from everything that contaminates body, and spirit,

…perfecting that holiness of faith, in our reverence and respect for, and our infatuation with, the love of God!"

Colossians 3:1 & 2

"If (or since) *then you __are__ rais__ed__ with Christ,*

…__set your mind then__ on the things that are __above__;

...set your mind on the things, on the greater realities of the Spirit,

...not on things that are on the earth;

...not on the flesh!"

...because you see, while your mind is on the things of the earth, *earthly;*

...while your mind is on the things of the flesh, your fleshly, natural existence, your natural identity in the flesh,

...you cannot submit to the law of the Spirit of life in Christ Jesus!

...therefore you cannot walk at liberty!

...you cannot walk in the freedom in which Christ has already set you free!

...therefore you continue to walk in sin!

...you continue to walk in death!

...you continue to walk in condemnation!

...you continue to walk in fear!

...you continue to walk in anxiety!

...you continue to walk in embarrassment!

...*and you continue to <u>be</u> an embarrassment!*

...*a poor excuse for a Christian!*

...*and all the forces of darkness still have their hold on you, and they work within you!*

There actually is only three things that the enemy can use against you, *to nullify the law of the Spirit of life in Christ Jesus!*

The number one thing is, if you continue to sin, ***by keeping your mind occupied with sin!***

If you do that, then you can listen to the best, most powerful teaching there is,

...and you can even have the most powerful experiences with God in your past,

...but if you do that,

...if you continue to set your mind on sin,

...*then you nullify the law of the Spirit of life in Christ Jesus,*

...*and you will continue to be bound by those demons you entertain in your thought-life!*

The number two thing the enemy uses against you, *to nullify the law of the Spirit of life in Christ Jesus,* **is ignorance!**

If you don't know any better; if you just don't know any better; if you are oblivious to the implications of the things you are getting involved with and submitting yourself to,

…I mean, if you think you can handle it, but you don't know and don't realize that you are already in trouble, *and you are ignorant to the power of sin,*

…then my friend, *the enemy has you right where he wants you,* **and that law of the Spirit of life in Christ Jesus will not operate.**

It cannot operate in an environment of ignorance!

And then, the number three thing the enemy uses *to nullify the law of the Spirit of life in Christ Jesus* **is disobedience!**

It's just pure old disobedience;

…**failing to put the knowledge of God to work for you!**

I mean, **you know the truth!**

…**BUT** you prefer **not to implement it**!

You choose not to walk in it!

You choose to deceive yourself!

You choose to live a lie!

And then, my friend, **you cannot even blame the devil**, *because <u>you yourself</u> nullify the law of the Spirit of life in Christ Jesus!*

Romans 8:7,

"...for the mind set on the flesh, on your natural identity, on your natural existence only, is hostile to God; it does not submit to God's law; it refuses to!"

"...therefore that person cannot walk in the law of the Spirit of life in Christ Jesus!"

This is the experience of many many people, *Christians even;*

...the law of the Spirit of life does not work for them,

...because their mind is SET on the things of the flesh,

...and so they cannot help but have the experience of failure they are having!

Many many Christians are still living in this experience of failure!

And that is precisely why they so often also wrongly interpret Romans 7 and associate what Paul is saying there with *life as a Christian,*

…**but Paul is not talking about life as a Christian there,** *he is talking about life under the Law!*

True Christianity is the furthest thing from that kind of experience!

Romans 8:8,

*"**Those who are in the flesh** (...trapped in a mind SET on the flesh, on their natural existence, on their natural identity,) ...**they cannot please God!**"*

Verse 9 says,

*"...**but you are not in the flesh**!*

(You are not trapped in that old mentality, that natural oriented mindset!)

You are in the Spirit!"

You are new creations in Christ Jesus' work of redemption!

 You are not in the flesh!

'But, brother Rudi, what about this body of mine?'

'What does he mean, "You are not in the flesh?"'

Listen you are in the Spirit,

...because you are spirit!

These redemption truths; these redemption realities *directly apply to you!*

"You are in the Spirit, if in fact the Spirit of God dwells in you!"

In other words, *if that spirit of TRUTH dwells in you;*

...if God's TRUTH dwells in you;

...if you have embraced redemption <u>realities</u> <u>as truth</u> in your heart and become <u>convinced</u> of it,

...then the Spirit of Truth, the Spirit of God Himself; God in all His fullness, dwells in you, *<u>by that truth you have embraced</u>!*

"...anyone who does not have the Spirit of Christ; that Spirit of Truth,

...that person does not <u>belong</u> to Him!"

...that person has not found the TRUTH yet, they have not found <u>their place of belonging</u> in Him!

Listen God rejects no one!

If you reject that redemption truth, *then it is you who rejects God, not God who rejects you!*

194

The new birth; the <u>birth of truth</u> in you; the <u>birth of faith</u>, brings the Holy Spirit to you!

...it brings God's <u>indwelling</u> to you!

That is what the new birth is all about!

That new birth of <u>faith</u> in your spirit brings the <u>Spirit LIFE</u> of Christ into your spirit!

It <u>awakens</u> and <u>activates</u> your spirit!

It <u>awakens</u> and <u>activates</u> the new creation!

It <u>awakens</u> and <u>activates</u> that dormant man that was created according to God in His image and likeness!

The birth of faith <u>awakens</u> and <u>activates</u> that new man!

...<u>that new expression</u> of God's image and likeness!

That new man was created in Christ Jesus!

It was created <u>according to God</u>,

...in righteousness and true holiness;

...in the holiness of truth! - Ephesians 4:24

And that new man *was <u>awakened</u> and <u>brought forth in you</u>,*

...in the new birth of the Spirit of truth and faith _that has come into your heart, to dwell and to abide there, as you embrace Him!_

...as you embrace His word;

...as you embrace His truth;

...as you embrace the gospel;

...as you embrace redemption and reconciliation and new creation realities!

(That other experience of the baptism of the Holy Spirit **is to equip you for ministry,** _so that the gifts of the Spirit and the workings of the Spirit can work and flow through you **in greater measure,**_

...**and manifest through you powerfully** _and more effectively!_)

Romans 8:10,

"...anyone who does not have the Spirit of Christ does not belong to Him,

...has not found their place of belonging in Him,

...but if (since) Christ is in you, although your body is dead because of sin, your spirit is alive because of righteousness"

Now we read verse 10 and we think,

'Well, that must mean that my body is still dead;

…still under the dominion of death and of sin;

…still under the law of sin and death!'

No, no, no!

Listen you have to read this whole discussion as one giant topic Paul was writing on.

That's why I can't just cut things short,

…and that's why this book ended up thicker than I had planned and wanted it to be at first.

This discussion of Paul started way back in Chapter 1 already; we just picked it up somewhere in the middle.

Remember it was a letter that Paul wrote.

It is all just one giant truth that we are breaking down and reading portions of.

But when Paul wrote it, there were no chapters and verses used… ha… ha… ha…

…not even capital letters and stops and commas and the whole works we use in our English language and in our Bibles.

You almost have to read this whole extensive discussion; this whole enormous truth, from the beginning and as a whole, in order for you to understand it thoroughly,

...before you can interpret Romans 8:10 correctly... ha... ha... ha...

...or the whole of Chapter 7 and Chapter 9 for that matter!

Chapter 21

Conclude yourself dead to sin!

Where did the death of your body come from?

I mean, here in Romans 8:10, where he says,

*"…**although your bodies are dead** (…***not because of***, but a better translation would be: **in regards to**) **sin**…"*

Where did that death *"**in regards to sin**"* come from?

Where did that death to sin in your body come from?

Where did that death to sin come from?

Listen he is not referring to *"the body of death"* talked about in Romans 7!

He is referring to *"the body of death"* talked about in Romans 6!

So, where does that death to *"the body of sin"* come from?

Romans 6:11

"Consider yourself dead to sin therefore!"

Another translation says,

"Reckon yourself, therefore, dead to sin!"

In other words,

"Come to a correct mathematical equation!"

"Come to an accurate conclusion!"

Come to an accurate conclusion therefore, concerning these things, in light of the fact that, when He died, *you died!*

You died there with Him;

…that old man of sin died!

And when Jesus was raised, *you were raised with Him!*

When He was raised, *you were raised a new creation!*

You were raised to newness of life!

You were raised to freedom!

Because *"that body of death;"*

"…the body of sin;"

…the power of sin and death

…was broken there!

Resurrection LIFE is now your portion!

He says,

Romans 6:11

"Reckon yourself, therefore, indeed dead to sin,

…and alive to God!"

Hallelujah!

So, let's read Romans 8:10 correctly now,

"Anyone who does not have the Spirit of Christ does not belong to Him, but if Christ is in you, (*…or* **since** Christ is in you) *although your body is dead in regards to sin, your spirit is alive because of righteousness"*

Let's go back to Romans 6 quickly so I can put this in proper context.

Let's read from verse 4,

"We were buried therefore, with Him, by immersion into death"

Remember that **Jesus partook of flesh and blood, in order to partake of death,** *in order to destroy the power of death!*

Why?

So that we don't need to die that death anymore!

"We were buried therefore with Him in that baptism of death,

...so that as Christ was raised from the dead,

...we too, by the glory of the Father,

...we too, might live in newness of life

...and walk in newness of life!"

Verse 5,

"For if we have been united with Him, in the same death, we are most certainly united also, with Him, in the same resurrection!"

Now listen, verse 6 says,

"We know that our old self was crucified with Him, so that the sinful body (...or that whole body of sin; that whole thing; that whole old deceived mindset) *might be destroyed!"*

"...so that the body of sin; the body of death might be destroyed!"

You have to see how Paul takes his argument, and he approaches it and discusses it from different angles.

In Chapter 7, he cries out in verse 24,

"Wretched man that I am who will deliver me from this body of death?"

But now he says in Romans 6 that, through our faith in Christ Jesus, we reckon our body dead to sin!

He says,

"…a dead man cannot be tempted by sin!"

He says,

"Now we reckon our body dead to sin!"

We say to sin, *'Sin, my body is no longer available to you! I am dead as far as you are concerned!*

…For I have been crucified in Christ; I have been crucified with Christ,

…nevertheless I LIVE!"

Romans 6:6,

"We are crucified with Him,

...so that the sinful body might be destroyed,

...and we might no longer be enslaved to sin!"

"...so that we might no longer be enslaved to sin!"

That means that dominion of the law of sin and death, *it's finally broken!*

You no longer *need to be* enslaved to sin!

Isn't that powerful!

Romans 8:10

"...although your bodies are dead because of sin..."

Why is the body dead now?

Because of sin!

...because you do not want to allow sin,

...and because you no longer *need to* allow sin in your body!

...you don't *need to!*

...because you have reckoned it, dead; you have reckoned and considered your body, dead!

You have come to the right conclusion in the gospel!

You have totally considered the truth and accurately reckoned your body, dead to sin!

You have identified yourself with Jesus Christ in His death,

…so you are no longer available for sin in the flesh!

"…but your spirit is now alive because of righteousness!" – Romans 8:10

…because of the birth of truth in your heart!

…because of the new birth of faith in your heart!

…because that faith and that truth have given birth to the new creation;

…to that new expression in your life!

…that expression of your original design and your true identity as child of God!

…His image; His likeness; His love now on display in your life!

…there is a new expression of the Christ-LIFE now awakened and brought forth in your life! Hallelujah!

*"...**your spirit is alive, because of righteousness!**"*

That new birth means, you are righteous!

You see, Paul's argument, Paul's reasoning in the truth of the gospel still continues,

...and the climax comes now here in verse 11

Romans 8:11,

*"...**if the Spirit of Him who raised Jesus from the dead dwells in you**..."*

Now verse 9 already confirms that fact!

He dwells in you!

Because you have <u>believed</u> the truth of redemption, He dwells in you!

You are in the Spirit; you have access to that dimension; to the dimension of the Spirit of God, *because you are a spirit!*

So He is already there; *He has access to your spirit!*

So He's in you, *but now He comes to abide in you and make His home with you!*

Through the truth of the gospel;

...through the truth of redemption,

*…*He comes to dwell in you, in overflowing fullness!

Romans 8:11

"…if (or since) **the Spirit of Him who raised Jesus from the dead dwells in you** (*…*through **the truth** of the gospel; through **your embrace** of **the truth** of the gospel; through your **believing the truth** of the gospel)**, He who raised Christ Jesus from the dead will give life to your mortal** (or dead) **body _also_, through His Spirit which dwells within you now!"**

Do you see how **there is an impartation of life now, even in my body?**

There is a strengthening, not just physically as far as my health is concerned, that too,

*…***but there is a supernatural strengthening in my spirit and my soul and therefore in my physical body;**

…an enablement against sin!

I want you to picture that so clearly,

Alright, now here I am, in my body I've been a servant of sin! I've been fighting, and I've been hating people with my tongue and my actions and whatever else, and I've been ugly and addicted to this, that, and the other thing;

I've been doing all the things that the body can possibly do in sin!

My faculties and my members; my mind and the members of my body were *enslaved* to sin!

There was a definite power at work there, a government, a powerful influence and rule and dominion.

Sin used my mind and my crooked thinking and my warped beliefs and my person, and the members of my body to fulfill its purposes!

Now I hear the truth of the gospel!

The gospel comes; truth comes; faith comes *and I am transformed by that impartation of words; by that impartation of faith and truth; by that renewing of my mind and that impartation of Spirit and by that impartation of LIFE!*

...and now I reckon myself dead!

But, now I'm not just dead!

...a dead dummy or a dead manikin for all eternity!

...alive in the spirit,

...but here my body is, just a stiff corpse!

I'm just dead you know!

No!

The Spirit of Him that raised Jesus from the dead quickens my mortal (...my dead) body;

...He affects even my natural man;

...my soul and my body!

There is a <u>quickening</u>;

...an <u>awakening</u>,

...an <u>activation</u> in my spirit,

...and even my body comes <u>alive</u> for God!

And so, suddenly I am prepared for service!

The members of my body now become servants *of my <u>awakened and quickened spirit</u>;*

...servants of righteousness!

Now I can begin to work righteousness!

This mind that used to think evil *can now think righteousness!*

This tongue that used to speak gossip and deception and all kinds of lies and

manipulation and junk and evil, *now speaks life!*

The members of my body *now serve Christ Jesus and righteousness!*

Do you see that?

Now I believe this is but a small part of what that immersion into Christ; into the body of Christ, and that quickening, and awakening, and activation of the Holy Spirit, in my spirit, is all about!

It's the beginning of the baptism of the Holy Spirit!

…only the beginning of that immersion into the glory of God, and into the fullness of God!

Romans 8:12,

*"…**so then brethren, so then, we are debtors, not to the flesh, to live according to the flesh!***"

(…if you want to, you can write there in your Bibles also, in completion of that thought,)

*"…**but we are debtors to the Spirit, to live according to the spirit!***"

Paul did what I do sometimes; he got so excited *he didn't finish his thought!* Ha… ha… ha…

…now don't frown at me,

…I saw you do that!

Ha… ha… ha…

…relax Max!

(*…and for a list of all my jokes people don't get, talk to my wife… ha… ha… ha…*)

Verse 13,

*"…**for if you live according to the flesh, you will die!**"*

…you will continue in death;

…you will continue under the law of sin and death!

(Remember verse 7 and verse 8, he is simply referring you back to that thought now)

*"…**if you live according to the flesh, you will die,***

*…**<u>BUT</u>, if by the spirit, you put to death the deeds of the body,***

*…**you will live!**"*

*…**you will truly LIVE!***

Verse 14,

"…for all who are led by the Spirit of God are sons of God!"

Chapter 22

Led by the Spirit of God

When are you led by the Spirit?

When the Truth of redemption, when the truth of the new Creation, when the truth of your original design and true identity, as a child of God, being in His image and likeness, *is submitted to;*

*…**when that law of the Spirit of life in Christ Jesus, is submitted to,***

*…**when you bow the knee *to the truth of God,***

*…**when you bow the knee to law and the government of the Spirit of life,***

*…then suddenly, **that government comes into power!***

*…it comes into **affect!***

…and what does that government do?

That government begins to lead you, and begins to show you, and begins to speak to you,

…and you see, then the Word, *the Spirit of the Word,* begins to be the motivation of your life,

…and you are led by the Spirit of Truth;

…by the Holy eternal Spirit Himself;

…the very person of God!

"For where the Spirit of the Lord is, there is liberty!" – 2Corinthians 3:17

Romans 8:15-17

"For you did not receive the spirit of slavery to fall back into fear!"

"…but you have received the Spirit of sonship whereby we cry, 'ABA' *Father,* (or DADDY God!)*"*

"It is the Spirit Himself who bears witness with my spirit, that, we are indeed children of God"

"Now since we are indeed children of God, then we are heirs of God – co-heirs, fellow heirs with Christ!"

Go with me just quickly to Romans 6:11 & 12

Verse 11,

"Reckon and consider yourselves dead to sin, and alive to God!"

That means I'm not just now *unproductive.*

No!

"Present yourself then, a living sacrifice!" says Paul in Romans 12:1 & 2.

That means being alive *unto God,*

…being alive, spirit, soul and body,

ALIVE!

God doesn't want anything *dead;*

…dead works; dead sacrifices!

He wants you *alive in the spirit,*

…alive unto Him,

…totally ALIVE!

Life more abundantly!

If He wanted you dead, and in Heaven, He would have struck you with lightning or something; He would have killed you and *taken you out of here, the moment you believed the gospel,*

…but no!

*…**God doesn't want you dead!***

*…**He wants you alive!***

God's got function in mind for you!

He's got service in mind for you!

But now He wants YOU *to present* YOUR BODY a *LIVING* sacrifice! Amen!

He says,

Romans 6:12,

*"**Let not sin, therefore, <u>reign</u> in your mortal (dead) *body!*"*

Can you see the body is dead?

*…***it is just a glove,**

*…***it is ready to serve the hand;**

*…***it is ready to serve <u>you</u> now,**

*…***and do what <u>you</u> want it to do *in your spirit.***

He says,

Verse 12,

*"**Therefore let not sin <u>reign</u> in your body!**"*

He is speaking to a person who understands that they are a new creature.

He says in essence,

'Listen, don't let the devil deceive you now,

…so that sin continues to reign and rule in your life!

…Its reign and rule is broken!

…Let it not continue!'

You see, God would never say to you, *"Let not…"* **if it was not possible!**

God says, *"Let not…"*

…because He knows it is more than possible,

…in fact, *it is more than reasonable* **for Him to expect it of you,**

…because He has made it available to you;

…He has given it as a gift to you!

"It's your reasonable contribution"

…your reasonable, logical conclusion, and contribution in life;

…in your body!

Hallelujah!

He has given it as a gift to you!

It's your legal right *to be free from the reign and rule of sin in your body!*

Romans 6:12

"Let not sin, <u>*therefore,*</u> <u>*reign*</u> *in your mortal body to make you obey its passions!"*

Verse 13,

"Do not yield your members to sin, as instruments of wickedness,

…but yield yourself to God!"

You see, the devil would just love to, *and sin would just love to…*

*…*the enemy wants to; *it wants to use your mind to think through, and your body to act through, and express itself through.*

"…but yield yourself to God, as a person who has been brought back from death to life, and therefore, yield also your members to God, as instruments of righteousness!"

Verse 14,

"…for sin will have no dominion over you!"

218

Hallelujah!

Verse 19,

"For just as you once yielded your members to impurity, and greater and greater iniquity, so now, yield your members to righteousness, as fruit of your sanctification"

Verse 16 says,

"Do you not know, that, if you yield yourself to anyone as an obedient slave, you are an actual slave of the one whom you obey, either of sin, which leads to death,

…or you can become addicted and obedient to truth, which leads to righteousness!"

Another translation says,

"…you can yield to sin, which leads to death, or you can yield to the obedience of faith, which is righteousness!"

(Faith's obedience means righteousness; *believing you are righteous, and yielding to that!***)**

(Note: This is a reference to Romans 1:16 where Paul talks about **the obedience of faith**. He says there that it is the preaching of the gospel that brings about that kind of obedience; that kind of faith. Our faith now, and our obedience now, are synonymous. Our faith is our obedience. That faith is what obedience is all about.)

Verse 17,

*"**Thanks be to God, that you, who once were slaves of sin, <u>has become obedient from the heart</u>, to the standard of teaching, to which you have been committed** (...and by which you have been delivered)"*

*"...<u>**has become obedient form the heart**</u>"* **means, you have believed** *"...the standard of teaching* **(or the truth)** *to which you have been committed"*

In other words, you have been delivered by that truth, and by faith in that truth!

The next verse, Romans 6:18 tells us exactly what *"...that standard of teaching"* is; **the accurate truth of it!**

Verse 18,

*"**You have been set free, from sin, and have become addicted to righteousness; love-slaves of righteousness!**"*

Hallelujah!

*...***not the spirit of slavery!**

...**you have not become addicted to slavery, *but the spirit of sonship!***

...you have become addicted to the concept and life of sonship!

It means that my obedience is no longer a legalistic obedience, like it was under the Law.

My obedience now is not a legalistic obedience, as under the law; it is not a legalistic obedience!

I am no longer under compulsion!

...motivated and driven and enslaved by obligation!

No!

Thank God!

But I am walking in relational obedience!

...<u>love's</u> own yielding and obedience and trust!

It's our delight to obey Him!

It's our delight to obey the Spirit of sonship!

It's our delight to submit to the law of the Spirit of life in Christ Jesus!

Hallelujah!

Praise the Lord!

Thank you Jesus!

In closing, I urge you to get yourself a copy of *"The Mirror Bible"* available online at: www.friendsofthemirror.com or at www.amazon.com and several other book sellers.

If you want me or someone a part of our team to come to where you are, *anywhere in the world,* and give a talk or teach you and some of your friends *about the gospel message and these redemption realities,* simply contact us at www.livingwordintl.com *…*or you can always find me on www.facebook.com

If your life has changed as a result of reading this book, *please write to me and let me know.*

I would love to share your joy,

…so that my joy in writing this book may be full!

"That which was from the beginning,

which we have heard
(**with our spiritual ears**),
which we have seen
(**with our spiritual eyes**),
which we have looked upon
(**beheld, focused our attention
upon**),
and which our hands have also
handled
(**which we have also
experienced**),

concerning the Word of life,

we declare to you,

**that you also may have this
fellowship with us;**

**and truly our fellowship is with
the Father
and with His Son Jesus Christ.**

And these things we write to you
that your joy may be full."

~ 1 John 1:1-4

About the Author

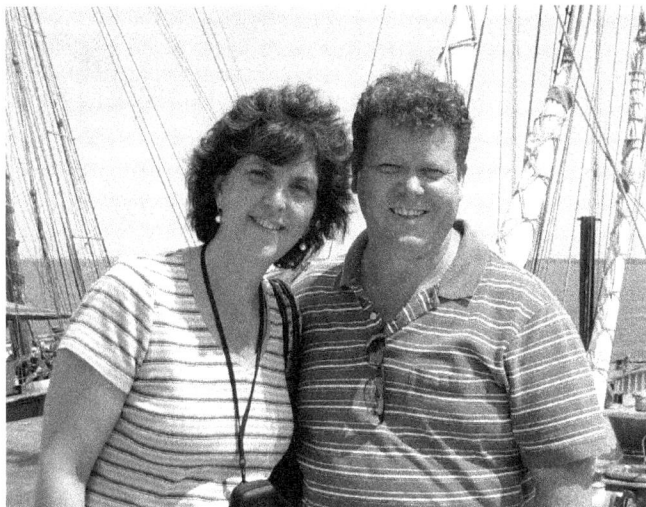

Rudi & Carmen Louw together oversee and pastor a church: Living Word International.

They also travel and minister both locally and internationally.

Rudi was born and raised in the country of South Africa while Carmen grew up in Cortland, New York.

They function in the ministry of reconciliation (2Corinthians 5:18-21) and flow strongly in the gifts of the Holy Spirit and His anointing to teach, preach, prophecy, heal and whatever is needed to touch peoples lives with the reality of God's love and power.

God has given them keen insight into what He has to say to mankind in the work of redemption, concerning the revelation of, and restoration of, humanity's true identity, and therefore, they emphasize THE GOSPEL; IN CHRIST REALITIES; the GRACE of God; the WORD OF RIGHTEOUSNESS *and all such eternal truths essential to salvation and living of the CHRIST-LIFE.*

They have been granted this wisdom and revelation into the knowledge of God, by the resurrected Spirit of Jesus Christ, *to establish and strengthen believers in the faith of God, and to activate them in ministering to others.*

Not only are people set free from the poison and bondage of sin, condemnation and all kinds of intimidation, (upheld, strengthened and reinforced by age old religious ideas born out of ignorance,) but many are brought into a closer more intimate relationship with Father God, as Daddy, through accurate teaching, and unveiling of the gospel message, prophetic words, healings and miracles.

Rudi & Carmen are closely knitted together with several other effective Christians, church fellowships, and groups of believers who share the same revelation and passion.

www.ingramcontent.com/pod-product-compliance
Lightning Source LLC
Chambersburg PA
CBHW051822090426
42736CB00011B/1610